Mayflies
"Top to Bottom"

SHANE STALCUP

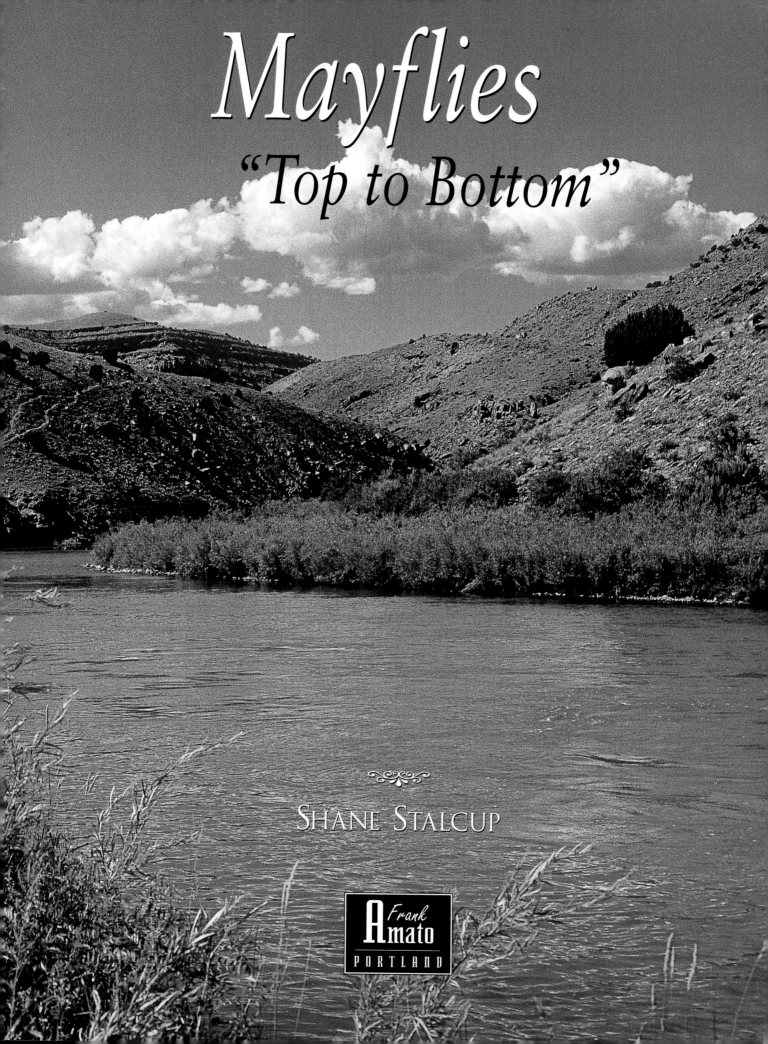

Mayflies
"Top to Bottom"

SHANE STALCUP

Frank Amato
PORTLAND

DEDICATED TO:

Mom and dad for all of their support and help as well as one of the families friends Ed Macavoy. It was his enthusiasm for matching the hatch and tying flies that placed an amber that has never dimmed. My only hope is that dad can understand what is presented.

Published in 2002 by Frank Amato Publications, Inc.
P.O. Box 82112, Portland, Oregon 97282
(503) 653-8108 • www.amatobooks.com

Softbound ISBN: 1-57188-242-1 • Softbound UPC: 0-66066-00496-3
Spiral Hardbound ISBN: 1-57188-243-X • Spiral Hardbound UPC: 0-66066-00497-0

All photographs taken by author except where noted.

Front Cover photograph: Toshi Karita
Frontispiece photograph: Brian O'Keefe
Title Page photograph: Shane Stalcup
Contents Page photograph: Brian O'Keefe

Book Design: Tony Amato

Printed in Singapore

10 9 8 7 6 5 4 3 2 1

CONTENTS

INTRODUCTION

This book is an accumulation of 20-plus years of commercial fly-tying experience and fly-fishing observations. During these years, virtually every fly style has passed through the jaws of my vise. The list includes: Humpies, Wulffs, standard dries, Trudes, nymphs, spinners, and emergers. Tying these different types of flies exposed me to many tying techniques and materials.

After several years of tying only the standard patterns, Michael Fong approached me at a sports show and asked, "Why don't you start creating your own flies?" A simple and obvious thought, but one that had yet to cross my mind. The rest is history, as they say.

We all have at least one person we can thank for having influenced our life experiences. Colorado's pool of talented fly tiers did just that for me. Extraordinary tiers such as John Betts, A.K. Best, Mike Tucker, Tim England, and Chuck Vestale to name a few are fellow tiers from which I have benefited. Each of these specialists, along with exposure to just about every fly-tying material made, gave me all I needed when I began the first of my creations.

When it comes to creating new patterns some tiers take the approach of imitation and others, including myself, go the way of realism. To make the fly look real does not mean tying in individual legs, eyes, and a mouth. The lifelike features come from carefully choosing materials for various parts of the fly. For example, the body of any mayfly is segmented which is why I use a lot of goose biots and micro tubing for this body part. These materials are far more realistic than a body dubbed with muskrat fur. The choice of material however can only come when one first knows what the fly looks like.

When we look at naturals on the water we see the top or side view. Since it's the fish we are trying to entice, we should look at what the insect looks like from the underside, as the trout do. This can be done by looking at photos or catching the naturals and studying them. Looking at the underside of the natural is still not enough as insects pass through various angles of a fish's vision. This is commonly referred to as the "fish's window." Keep in mind that since a trout's eyes are on the sides of its head, their field of vision is greatly increased. They can see food or prey below them, above them, to the sides, and behind them.

When our flies drift over the trout, certain aspects of the fly come into focus first, followed by the whole fly. With this in mind, take your fly and hold it at arm's length above your head. Hold your arm as far to one side as possible as you focus straight ahead. Then, move your arm across your field of vision. Do this slowly, increasing the speed to mimic the speed of the

river. Take notice of which parts of the fly are prominent; this may be tails, segmented body, tall wings, legs, or a large thorax. This simple exercise will give you a new perspective on how to construct your flies and that is how most of the flies in this book were developed.

The above exercise is great for developing dry flies but what about nymphs? Again, information from books and photos is priceless and a home aquarium doesn't hurt either. When out on the stream, roll over a few rocks and dislodge some of the nymphs into a waiting net. Once they are in the net, place them back into the water. While you do this, pay close attention to how the nymphs act. This can be observed more closely by placing the bugs in a cup of water. Whether in the stream or in a cup, observe how the nymph moves and again, notice its prominent features. With these exercises you will achieve a new insight into fly construction. These activities tell you how important wings are, for example, for an adult pattern, or the value in tying slender nymphs.

There is one more thing the fly tier should keep in mind while creating flies. That is, how is this fly going to act on or in the water? The current of the water will add some movement to your fly but the angler can also play a part. As the fly goes downstream, try moving the rod tip in various ways, this can be as simple as lifting the rod or merely pumping it. These movements can bring life to your fly by effecting how the materials act in the water. As the fly moves down river, the materials will lay along the sides of the fly while under tension but if the fly is allowed to briefly rest, certain materials will come alive.

The flies you will soon see were created for the hatches that occur throughout the Rocky Mountain States: Colorado, New Mexico, Wyoming, Montana, and Idaho. However, changing the color and sizes of the examples will allow you to match any hatch that you encounter. One of the hardest things for fly tiers to explain about a fly is their color. This is especially true when it comes to pale morning duns. They can range from olive/yellow, yellow/olive, light olive, pink, or a peach color. To help you along with this color spectrum, I have included some color chips along with the species of insect which it is meant to represent. Keep in mind that whatever material you use will get darker when it gets wet.

These thoughts and actions are what I run through when trying to create new patterns. As you will see, many chapters will again stress the importance of knowing what the naturals look like. This along with knowledge of all the various fly-tying materials is what makes creating flies fun and productive.

Chapter 1

TOOLS

There are numerous tools for the fly-tier but most have been discussed in other books, including bobbins, hair stackers, hackle guards, and bodkins. Following are the few that I find most valuable.

Vise: Although some people tie flies in their hands, a vise makes life a whole lot simpler. I first started with an Indian vise which lasted all of two flies and then I moved on to a Thompson. Wanting a vice that would hold small hooks securely, I purchased my first HMH vise. To this day, I am still using that same vise. When you figure that this vise has seen between 500,000 to 700,000 flies and it is still in top form, I don't think I will be looking for a new vice any time in the near future.

The best thing about the vise, besides its longevity, is its interchangeable jaws. If I am tying only small flies (18-24), I use the midge jaw. If the day calls for streamers, the saltwater jaws are used. Once these jaws latch on to your hook you'll never have to worry about them slipping out. Plus, it has a lifetime guarantee.

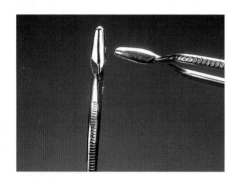

Hackle Pliers: Believe it or not, this simple little tool can make the difference between a good or bad experience when using them for wrapping biots. Since goose biots are fairly small to begin with, you do not need a pair of pliers which have to grab practically the whole biot. The best ones are the plain-old hackle pliers with a rounded point. They usually come in small and medium sizes, medium being my favorite. They are cheap and are the best for working with biots. The pliers with the rubber grips should be used for what they were intended, hackles.

Scissors: There is nothing worse than trying to cut something when your scissors will not go through it. A sharp pair of scissors can make tying a whole lot of fun, or if they are dull, one big headache. I like serrated scissors because they grab on to and hold the material being cut. I have had a pair of Dr. Slick scissors for some time now and haven't found any better.

In order to keep your scissors in top shape, it helps if they are used correctly. When cutting wire, use the back or meaty portion of the blades to do your cutting. For cutting the center stem out of feathers such as partridge, use the tips of the scissors for more control.

If you tie a lot of small flies you already know how hard it is to pick up small hooks from your desk. To make this task simpler, magnetize your scissors. This is done by rubbing the scissors tips across a magnet. If you happen to have tungsten scissors though, this will not work as this material is more stone than metal.

Sharpening Scissors: To help keep my scissors in top form (sharp), I sharpen them at least once a week. I use a ceramic knife sharpener. Put the ceramic stick in the end of the block, place one blade on the stick and draw it towards you, sliding it down the stick. By doing this, your scissors will remain in top working order.

MATERIALS

The materials used to construct your flies should be selected carefully as they will add life to your final product. Examine the insect photos throughout this book, take notice of the various parts of the insect and how the materials that are used resemble that part of the natural. For example, the biot body gives the tier a colored body complete with ribbing and a taper. Each of these materials are used for specific reasons to make the fly look and act as close to the natural as possible.

Goose Biots: The stiff fibers that protrude from the leading edge of the primary feather are called biots. Biots come in left and right forms as they come from the right and left wings of the bird. To best use these feathers, pull one from the stem as opposed to cutting it off. This leaves the base of the biot intact, a notch is preserved to let you know which way you will be tying it in, and a little length is added to the feather.

If you were to tie the biot in by the tip, the notch will be facing left or right. The side of the biot with the notch is referred to as the smooth side and the other side is the fuzzy rib. So, depending on how you want your body to look—smooth or with a fuzzy rib—it will depend upon where the biot's notch is facing. If you start to wrap it forward, and you do not like what you see, take the biot off and flip it around for the desired look. You can also look at the tying tips section where this is shown in more detail.

Before you tie in the biot, it is suggested that you first moisten it in some fashion. (The biots are dry and brittle and will break if they are not first moistened.) This can be done by placing quills onto a damp towel or by placing them into your mouth.

Once the biot is tied in, it is ready to be wrapped forward. Goose biots are not all that long, so every little bit has to be spared. This is where the right kind of hackle pliers is worth its weight in gold. Do not use the ones that have round rubber pads because you have to put too much of the biot into the jaws before they can get a grip. Remarkably, the best pliers are usually the cheapest ones. They are entirely metal and have the finest tip. (I am still using my first pair which cost about a dollar!)

What makes the goose biot a desirable body, is its segmentation. Just by wrapping the biot forward, you will have created a body complete with segmentation unlike any other material you have ever used. When dyed, the colors of the fat portion are solid and non-transparent, while the edge is dark. A neat little trick to darken the edge of the ribbing is to take a marker across the top of the biot after it is wrapped. This fuzzy rib will soak up the marker while leaving the base color intact.

The limited hook sizes that you are able to use can be a problem. For the most part, the goose biot is best used for hook sizes 16 and smaller with an emphasis on smaller. The key is to seek out long biots of good quality just like you would your hackle. The best source for quality goose biots is Hareline Dubbin. They have hand-selected biots which come in all the major hatch colors.

Turkey Biots: Turkey, on the other hand, has some different qualities. When compared to goose feathers, the most noticeable difference will be that of length. In many cases, the turkey feather will be almost twice the length of the goose feather. Yet, there is a drawback.

The bulk of the turkey biot is somewhat transparent. If you desire a body which is smooth and segmented, this biot just doesn't work. You will be able to tie up to three ribbed segments and then the transparency will occur and the segmentation will disappear. But, if you like your bodies to have that fuzzy rib, then you will be in hog heaven!

Because of its additional length, an underbody made of turkey can also be formed before you wrap the biot forward. This will create a thicker body.

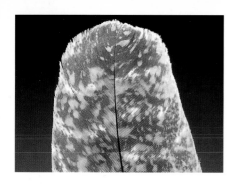

Ozark Mottled Turkey: In just about every nymph-tying situation, this material can be used for the wing case. The natural mottling of this feather is often imitated, but there is nothing like using the real thing. To make a more durable wing case, place some flexible glue on the shiny side of the feather. (The dull side will be placed on top because that is the side which has micro hairs on it.)

Ozark mottled turkey can also be used for a body material. Simply cut off a few fibers and then wrap them in order to create the body. The result will be fuzzy and mottled. When you have finished, you can then reverse wrap it with some wire for durability.

Ostrich: Ostrich plumes have numerous herls which stick out from their stems. On these long herls, small fibers protrude. These small, soft fibers are the part of the feather which will eventually bring the fly to life. They move nicely in the water, giving the appearance of gills.

Just like hackle though, ostrich plumes are not all the same. Some have fibers which are much longer then others. Because of this, it is a good idea to look at one out of the package before you buy it. Generally, the shorter the plume is, the shorter the fibers.

Once the herl is wrapped forward, some kind of reinforcement is needed for strength. This comes from ribbing it with wire, or by twisting the herl around your thread. The twisting of the herl, whether together with other colors, or around the thread, gives the herl a whole new appearance. Once it is twisted, the smaller fibers will stick out from the stem. This is important because once the herl is wrapped forward, you will want to rib it with something while trying not to tie down any of those small fibers.

Extended Bodies: Some of the prettiest and most exact patterns developed for mayflies include some kind of extended body. These flies can be tedious to tie because they usually take a fair amount of time to produce. Hareline Dubbin has solved this problem by producing some of the most realistic mayfly bodies available. They have separated tails which stay divided, and the body portion is segmented for the ultimate in realism. One of the nicer attributes of these bodies is that the clear or white ones can be made into whatever color you want. Just take a waterproof marker and color it.

To tie with them is a breeze. Just attach them to a short-shank hook and finish the fly however you wish. The Extended May shows one version you might like but don't stop there, try some other alterations as well like a parachute.

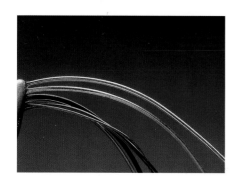

Tubing: Tubing is a product which has the appearance of similar products at first glance. When you begin to tie with it though, the differences become obvious. It has the elasticity of a rubberband and it will not turn yellow in the sun because of its UV protection. Its ablility to stretch though is what makes this material so special.

Depending upon the size of the flies that you are tying, tubing can work on just about any hook that you want. For example, the smallest of the three types, micro, can tie flies down to size 24. In addition, when tubing is cut at an angle, and then tied in by the tip, it can be stretched to fit all of your small-fly needs.

Tubing is also crystal clear and translucent which makes the body of a fly look more realistic in appearance. (The segmentations will appear second only to nature when wrapped.)

To add some variation, place some FisHair into the tubing before you wrap it, or simply wrap it between the creases. The segmentations will become even more pronounced with this little addition. To add some sparkle to your flies, try placing some Krystal Flash or Midge Flash into the tubing. Cut the flash at an angle and then place it into the tubing by twisting it.

The other two sizes, standard and midge, can be used for larger mayfly bodies. The standard is great for streamers, but for smaller mayflies, I would use the midge.

To create a tapered body with tubing, tightly stretch it for the first couple of wraps and then gradually release some of the tension. Working in this manner, the body will taper from the back to the front, and the segmentations will become more pronounced.

Most readers will probably want to use this material on their nymph patterns, but don't shy away from using it on dry flies as well. Since it is hollow, some air will get trapped inside of the tubing, helping the fly to float. In addition, another advantange is that when compared to a dubbed body, there is virtually no difference in weight.

Tubing comes in an array of colors so virtually any hatch can be matched. For an even more distinct look, use different colors of thread for the underbody before you wrap the tubing over it. (If you want a different color than what is available, use white thread and a waterproof marker on it.)

D-Rib: D-Rib is similar to tubing. It is made of the same stretchy material and is also UV protected. But the difference between the two materials will be seen when their shapes are compared after they have been wrapped. In a cross section, as the name implies, it is in the form of a "D."

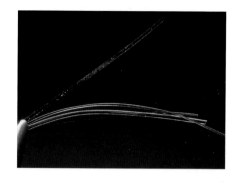

This translucent material is great for tying small mayfly nymph patterns such as the Baetis nymph. Like tubing, when you first start to wrap it, stretch it quite a bit. As you get further up, release some of the tension to build a more tapered body. Before you tie it in though, it is a good idea to first cut it at an angle. This way, you will not have a little hump when you wrap the rib over it.

D-Rib is a prominent ribbing material. Try tying a pheasant tail nymph and then rib it with the rust colored D-Rib. Just make sure that some of the pheasant tail fibers stick out in-between the ribbings. (This material is also fantastic when used with ostrich herl.)

No matter what color you may be looking for, there is one that is bound to fit your tying needs. But then again, if there isn't, use white thread, color it, and wrap some clear D-Rib over it.

It comes in two sizes: small and medium. (The medium can also be found with glitter. For a more realistic looking fly, this material will work.)

Similar products include Swannundaze and V-Rib. They all give that distinctive humped rib when wrapped, but D-Rib is the only one which can tie down to the twenties and once you try it, you will instantly see why I like this material so much.

Micro Dry-Fly Dubbing: When it comes to doing detail-oriented work, or tying small flies, this is the best dubbing for the job. (Besides, it is also treated with Water Shed fly floatant so you can go from the vise to the river without having to apply any fly floatant.) Additionally, it's one of the few dubbings that has been specifically blended to match the major hatches. This includes BWO's, PMD's, Red Quills, and for the first time Tricos.

It is so fine that you don't even have to put wax on your thread to create a tight body. However, if you want the tightest body possible, place some wax on your fingers before you start to twist the dubbing onto the thread.

Probably the greatest advantage is that the fibers are cut fairly short. This means that the novice tier won't be as likely to pull out too much dubbing from the package, trying unsuccessfully to place it on the thread. Therefore, this is a good material when tying small flies, because all that is needed is a small amount of dubbing.

Awesome Possum Dubbing: About the only time I use natural dubbing in my tying is when I am doing nymphs. For those larger mayfly nymphs, this stuff is great for the thorax. It comes complete with guard hairs and underfur to create some of the scraggliest, buggiest thoraxes you will ever see.

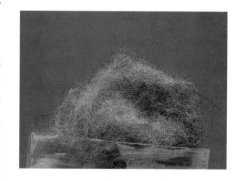

It is supple and easy to work with. On larger flies, a dubbing loop may be helpful because it speeds things up and can add a lot of bulk to your fly quickly. Once the thorax is created, pick out the guard hairs to give the illusion of legs. One of the best features Awesome Possum has over hare's mask, is that it doesn't trigger allergies so you won't have to reach for a Kleenex every two minutes.

Ice Dubbing: Every now and then a new material will leave you wondering how you ever lived without it. Ice Dubbing is one of these materials. Ice Dubbing is the finest reflective dubbing to date. You can dub it, use it for trailing shucks, use it for underwings, even for emerger wings.

Ice Dubbing is soft so it manipulates well between your fingers and on the thread. It comes in several great fish-catching colors but I like the ones with UV sparkle in them. When the light hits it, the fly instantly comes alive. Don't be afraid to use some on your saltwater flies.

Quick Descent Dubbing: This has to be one of the most original materials ever to come along, it is shredded aluminum. It does not stick in your fingers like metal shavings and feels soft to the touch. You will be amazed how small you can dub it.

Copper colored is my favorite, along with the copper Flashback. Once a dubbed body is formed, take a pair of needlenose pliers or hemostats and squeeze the body. The new body will be flat from top to bottom but wide from side to side. And, if your pliers have fine teeth, the squeezed body will be instantly ribbed. After the body is formed, take some clear tubing or D-Rib and wrap it over the body, then use the pliers. This way the body will hold its shape, or use some Zap-a-Gap for the same effect.

CDC: This has to be one of the easiest materials to work with, especially when it comes to tying small flies. There are a few things you should know about these feathers before they make a trip to the river with you.

Even though these feathers come from the preen gland area of the duck, it is not the oils from this area that help the feathers float. The flotation comes from the structure of the feather. Each fiber from the stem has tiny micro barbs on it. When these fibers are bunched up and placed on a hook, a tremendous amount of air is trapped within them. It's this air-trapping quality that gives these feathers their flotation. A good example of this is marabou. When you cast out your heavily weighted Woolly Bugger it floats. This fly will almost float forever if it's not pulled under the surface disturbing the marabou so that it gets wet. The marabou will float because of the air trapped in it and not because of oil.

The oil may not do all that much for the flotation but it does make the material more supple. This is important because many materials get dried out over time and become brittle. Today, many suppliers are having this preen oil put into all their natural materials for this reason. The oil on the CDC however does give it a quality that is somewhat unique. The oil gives a sheen to the feathers which can reflect light from various angles, making it look lifelike in the water. This is a great quality when tying wet flies.

Besides its floating qualities CDC can also be used on mayfly nymphs. The fibers come alive when they are pulled through the water and then followed by a pause. If you are using these magical little feathers for dry flies, remember not to put anything on them that will destroy their air-trapping qualities. Paste is a big no-no, as well as many silicone liquids. I like to use Top Ride or Blue Ribbon. These are both powder desiccants which work wonders on CDC flies or any dry flies for that matter. To dry the fly after it has become wet, dab it on your shirt sleeve and then place the fly into Easy Dry. It is a desiccant in the form of BBs. This way you will not get a bunch of powder sticking to your fly. There are other remedies for waterproofing and drying your flies but this is the system I find most effective.

Medallion Sheeting: This synthetic wing material is a take off from Zing Wing; it is slightly thicker and has permanent color. It is very strong cross ways but it will tear length ways. First determine how wide you want your wings to be and then cut it length ways to the width that you want. Once this is done, tie it in like a spinner wing, then any adult or emerger wing can be formed. To make life a little easier, take the strip of sheeting and twist it in the middle so that you have a nice tie-in point. With the wings tied down, pull each end of the wings to take out any slack.

The important thing to remember when using this material for upright wings is that the wings need to lay back at an angle so they will not twist your leader. This will not totally eliminate the problem, but just about any dry fly will twist your leader. I think it has a lot to do with how you cast and how windy it is. It's recommended that you not use Medallion sheeting for spinner wings. Yet, I have talked with individuals who do and have no problems.

Although it was designed for wings, Medallion sheeting has become indispensable when it comes to tying nymphs. This stuff is great for wing cases! When used in this fashion, you get a wet and glistening wing case that is very lifelike. When tying in this material, or any strip of material, start by holding the material on the side towards you. That way, when the thread is brought over the top, it will mold the material over the hook shank. As you will see on some of the spinner patterns, it is also great for holding down the wings and stray hackle fibers. It comes in an array of colors so any color you might need is available.

Saddle Hackle: These feathers are nice and long with a slim stem. It use to be that saddles were used only for streamers and larger dry flies. But out of the laboratories at Whiting Farms has come some of the most incredible dry-fly saddles we fly tiers have ever seen. These long feathers tie down to a size 20 and, in some cases, 22s. These smaller-sized hackles can be found in Whiting's new grade of saddles called midge size.

Since they are much more dense in fibers than feathers from a neck, a couple of turns of this stuff are all that is needed to hackle your flies. This means that 5, 6, 7, or even 12 flies can be tied from the same feather. Plus, since it is so long, the need for hackle pliers is a thing of the past, or at least until you get down to the very end.

One of the most exciting new additions to Whiting's line-up is hackle that is dyed to match some of the major hatches, including pale morning duns, blue-winged olives, *Callibaetis*, and March browns. Since hackle is meant to represent the legs of the fly, why not use the right color? Like the hatch-matching colors of Micro Dry Fly Dubbing.

Dry-Fly Necks: This particular material will send shock waves through your wallet when you see how much it costs. However, if you could see what is all involved in creating such high grade feathers, you would probably be a little more understanding. The process is unbelievable. These feathers are what is used on all my small flies, size 18-24. Saddles may work some of the time but to make sure that you have these smaller gems, it's a good idea to have a neck. A good dry-fly neck will tie an array of fly sizes ranging from 8-22. It's always a good idea to take a neck out of the bag to look at it before buying it.

Look for feather count, especially in the smaller sizes. Also be aware of tips that are broken off as you thumb through the cape. Take the time to bend a few of the feathers to see how they stick out from the stem. This can show if the cape has been properly cleaned of fats and oils. If a poor job has been done, the oils will migrate into the barbules and cause the fibers to stick together. Check the gaps between the fibers as well, if the gaps are too wide, pass up that neck.

Hen Necks: For the most part these necks have been used for wet flies, nymphs, and wings. We have been told time and again that stiff hackle is the only way to go when it comes to dry flies. What we have failed to realize is that hackle is used to support the fly by dispersing the weight through the hackle, and, to a lesser extent, imitating legs. Virtually any type of hackle will do this so why not use a lesser grade of feather and save some money?

There is no getting around it that stiff hackle is needed to fish in rough waters but on slower-moving waters the softer hen neck can be used. These feathers are especially useful when used on emerger and cripple patterns as you will see later on in the book. For the past couple of years I have been using them on most of my emergers and cripples and my success rate has gone up. I attribute this success to the softer feathers. They allow your fly to land more softly on the water and they add animation unlike the stiffer hackles.

Like most materials you get what you pay for and hen necks are no different. I particularly like Whiting's because of their length. When used on smaller flies, one feather can hackle a couple of flies. Plus, no one else has the Hebert hens which are so magnificently colored. All in all, this one tying material that I have become accustomed to, and am never without it.

Deer Hair: When deer hair is mentioned when tying mayflies, you generally think of big bushy flies like Wulffs and Humpys. In both cases, the hair is used for wings and in one instance a back strap. As for this book, deer hair is used for the legs of the fly.

Deer hair, from its base to its tip, provides a nice taper which makes it ideal for using it as legs. The hair is tied on the underside of the fly and left to flair out. With a few turns of the thread through it however confines this mess into a orderly appearance. Deer hair is perfect for this because of its natural taper. From the thorax, the hair tapers outwards to a fine point just like a natural's.

The type of hair really isn't all that important since basically only the tips are used. When buying deer hair make sure that the tips are not broken. Also look for changes in color from the tip down. By using the natural hair, you have the perfect color for a *Callibaetis* pattern.

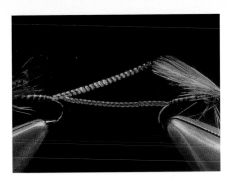

Trailing Shucks: We are all aware of using Z-lon and Antron for trailing shucks so I don't want to be redundant because there are a couple of other materials that are worth mentioning. Ice Dubbing, which has already been discussed in the dubbing section, and Hareline's Trailing Shucks.

These new trailing shucks are really worth looking at. They look so real I don't see how fish can refuse them. They are translucent, hollow pieces which come complete with segmentations. All you have to do is attach them to the hook shank and finish off the body however you wish. The most versatile color is clear. Since it is a synthetic it can be made any color with the help of a Chartpak marker.

Partridge: What would fly tiers do without this feather? The natural softness and coloration of these feathers is remarkable. Although the natural brown is most widely used, you can also get these feathers dyed in great fish-catching colors. Before you purchase a skin, take it out of the package to make sure that the skin is full and that the feathers are not damaged. For the best feathers with the least amount of damage, buying a skin is the way to go versus pre-packaged feathers.

Mayfly Tails: Also called Micro-Fibetts, these fibers were popularized by John Betts. They are synthetic-like hairs which taper to a point making them great for tails. They come pre-treated with Water Shed floatant. Their stiffness allows the tier to use only a few fibers for the tail so that it doesn't look like a horse's tail sticking out the back. They come in many different colors but if there were a color that is not available, take your Chartpak marker and make them what ever color you want.

A useful tip when using these fibers on cripples and emergers is to place them in a pair of hemostats to crimp them. The result is a segmented mangled tail which comes darn close to looking like the natural's.

Ultra Wire: For as long has time has been kept, we have all used gold or silver wire to reinforce our fly bodies. Now, we have a choice. From a multitude of colors we can pick which color goes best with the flies we are tying. This wire comes in small sizes for those micro patterns and continues up in size for larger flies. Besides adding strength, this colored wire can be used for creating the bodies themselves. The fly is weighted and a nice segmented body is formed, all in one step.

Flashback: Some of the most productive flies in use today incorporate some kind of flashy material for the wing case, including Flashabou and pearl sheeting material. Now, there is another choice, flashy pearl material which comes in various colors. Just cut a strip the width your wing case will be and tie it in. The nice thing about this material is that it is very thin so it can be used on small flies. Wait until you try the rust color on your Pheasant Tail Nymphs. The results are amazing. It's also great for wrapping a body, then covering it with the tubing of D-Rib.

FisHair: When it comes to ribbing flies, wire and thread are most often used. However, all the while there was a material available that was overlooked as a ribbing material. FisHair can be used to rib between the tubing or D-Rib wraps, or even put into the tubing for a more dramatic ribbing effect. With an endless range of colors, you should have no trouble finding a color that will fill your needs.

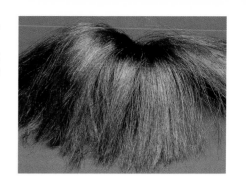

Waterproof Markers: For many years John Betts has talked of the importance of using markers in tying flies. A white fly can instantly be transformed into whatever color you desire. This is important to remember, especially when using synthetic materials. However, not all markers hold their weight. Nothing is more maddening than finding a color you like and then going back to the store to replace it only to find that the color has been discontinued. This happens with several brands but not Chartpak. For the past ten years or so, I have been using the same chartpak colors and have yet to come across this problem. Another advantage of this marker is its triangular tip. You can make a wide sweep of the marker for broad areas or you can use the tip for more precise applications. Whatever color you need, Chartpak will probably have it.

INSECT HOOK SIZE CHART

INSECT HOOK SIZE CHART							
Blue-Winged Olive:			16	18	20	22	
Pale Morning Dun:		14	16	18			
Callibaetis:		14	16	18			
Red Quill:		14	16	18			
Mahogany Dun:			16	18	20		
Sulphur:			16	18	20	22	
Baetis:			16	18	20	22	24
Trico:				18	20	22	24

Fly Tyer's Guide

Daiichi — Premium Fishing Hooks ®

Serious Hooks for Serious Anglers

General Description	Daiichi XPoint	Dai-Riki	Mustad	Orvis	Eagle Claw	Partridge	Tiemco
DRY FLY HOOKS							
Wide Gape, "Big" Down Eye	1100		80000BR	4864			100
Wide Gape, "Big" Straight Eye	1110		94859	4641			101
Standard	1170	300	94840	1876	59	L2A	5210
Standard, Mini-Barb	1180		94840	1523			5210
Barbless	1190		94845	1877	61	E3AY	
2X-Long Dry	1280	730	94831	1638		H1A	5212
1X-Short, Down Eye	1310	305	94838	1509			921
1X-Short, Up Eye	1330		94842		59		
Limerick, Mini-Barb	1480		94859	170T		K1A	
CURVED HOOKS							
Heavy Scud	1120/X120	135	80200BR				2457
Scud, Down Eye	1130		80250BR	1639	55	K4A	2487
Midge/Emerger	1140		80100BR	1639			206BL
Heavy Wide-Gape	1150		80200BR	8891	56		2457
Curved Shank	1270	270	80050BR	1510	52		200R
Chironomid	1273			161T			
WET/NYMPH HOOKS							
2X-Heavy Wet	1530	075	3908	1641			3769
Standard Wet	1550	070	3906	167T	57	G3A	
1X-Long Nymph	1560	060	3906B				3761
2X-Long Nymph, Down Eye	1710/X710	730	9671	1524	63	D4A	5262
3X-Long Nymph	1720	710	9672	1526	58		5263
Stonefly Nymph	1730	700B	81002BR				
Swimming Nymph	1770		80150BR	1512			400T
STREAMER HOOKS							
4X-Long, Straight Eye	1750		9674	0167		D3ST	9395
4X-Long, Down Eye	2220/X220	700	79580	8808	281	D4A	
6X-Long	2340		3665A	1511			300
Aberdeen, Black	2461		3262				
SALMON HOOKS							
Low Water	2421		90240	1644		N	7989
Traditional	2441	899	36890	1645		M	7999
Heavy Egg-Steelhead	2571/X510						105
Double Salmon	7131		80525BL	0528		Q	
SPECIALTY HOOKS							
Saltwater	2546/X452	930	34007	9034	254SS		811S
Stinger	2720		80300BR	8810			8089

This is a general reference guide of similar hook patterns

Angler Sport Group • 6619 Oak Orchard Road • Elba, NY 14058 • USA

www.anglersportgroup.com

Japanese Chemically Sharpened Hooks

Dry Fly Hooks

TAR 100
Dry fly - Down eye, 1 X fine wire, Wide Gape, Forged, Bronze #6 - 24

TAR 101
Dry fly, Straight eye, 1 X fine wire, Wide Gape, Forged, Bronze #8 - 24

TAR 103 *NEW! In 2003*
Dry fly, Down eye, Barbless, Extra fine wire, Wide Gape, Non-Forged, Bronze #8 - 22

TAR 104 BL *NEW! In 2003*
Dry fly, Down eye, Barbless, Extra Fine Wire, Bent-in point, Non-Forged, Black Nickel #10 - 20

TAR 921
Dry fly, Down eye, 1 X FIne, 2 X short, Forged Bronze #8 - 20

TAR 5212
Dry fly, Down eye, 1 X Fine 2 X Long, Perfect bend, Long shank, Forged Bronze #6 - 20

Nymph, Hopper & Terrestrials Hooks

TAR 3761
Nymph & Wet fly, Down eye, 2 X Heavy, 1 X Long, Sproat bend, Non Forged, Bronze #2 - 20

TAR 3769
Nymph & Wet fly, Sproat bend, 2 X Heavy, Non Forged, Bronzed #6 - 18

TAR 200
Dry Fly, Nymph and Terrestrial, Straight Eye, Standard Wire, 3 X Long, Semi-dropped Point, Forged, Bronze, #2 - 22

TAR 2302
Dry Fly and Terrestrial, Down Eye, Standard Wire, 2 X Long, Humped Shank, Forged Bronze #6 - 16

TAR 2312
Dry Fly and Terrestrial, Down Eye, 1 X Fine, 2 X Long, Humped Shank, Forged Bronze #6 - 16

TAR 5262
Dry Fly and Terrestrial, Down Eye, 1 X Fine, 2 X Long, Forged, Bronze, #6 - 16

Salt Water Stainless Steel

TAR 800S
Saltwater fly - Straight Eye, Heavy Wire, Semi-Drop Point, Forged, #4/0 - 8

TAR 812S
Straight Eye, 1X Long, Extra Strong, O'shaughnessy Bend, Forged, #6/0 - 14

TAR 4310
Up Eye, Heavy Wire, Reversed, Octopus Beak, Forged, #6/0 - 10

Shrimp, Scuds and Caddis Pupa

TAR 2457
Down Eye, 2 X Heavy, 2 X Wide, Curved Shank, Non Forged Bronze #6 - 18

TAR 2487
Down Eye, Fine Wire, 2X Wide, Curved Shank, Non Forged, Bronze, #10-24

TAR 2091 *NEW! In 2003*
Up Eye, Standard Wire, 1X Short Shank, Reversed, Forged, Bronze, #6 - 16

TAR 206 BL *NEW! In 2003*
Up Eye, Standard Wire, 1X Short Shank, Barbless, Non Forged, Black Nickel, #6 - 16

Streamer and Buggers

TAR 5263
Down Eye, 2X Heavy, 3X Long, Perfect Bend, Forged, Bronze, #2 - 20

TAR 9394
Straight Eye, 3X Heavy, 4X Long, Forged, Nickel Plated, # 2 - 10

TAR 9395
Straight Eye, 3X Heavy, 4X Long, Forged, Bronze Plated, # 2 - 10

TAR 300
Down Eye, Heavy Wire, 6X Long, Forged, Bronze, #2 - 20

Salmon & Steelhead

TAR 7979
Nymph and Wet Fly, Straight Loop Eye, Heavy Wire, Curved Shank, Forged, Black Nickel, #1 - 10

TAR 7989
Dry Fly, Turned Up Loop Eye, Light Wire, Forged, Black Nickel, #1/0 - 10

TAR 7999
Wet Fly, Turned Up Loop Eye, Heavy Wire, Forged, Black Nickel, # 2/0 - 12

Special Use Hooks

TAR 8089 *NEW! In 2003*
Bass Bugs and Mice, Straight Eye Stinger, Fine Wire, Extra Wide Gap, Forged Bronze, #2 - 12

TAR 105
Wet Fly and Glo Bug, Straight Eye, 2X Strong, 5X Short, Reverse Bend, Non Forged, Bronze, #4 - 10

TAR 8352 *NEW! In 2003*
Trailer Hook, 5 Degrees Up Eye, 1X Strong, Forged, Black Nickel, #1 - 6

TAR 3310 *NEW! In 2003*
San Juan Worm and Trailer Hook, Up Eye, 1X Strong, Forged, Black Nickel, #2 - 5

TAR 8626BL *NEW! In 2003*
Trailer Hook, Turned Down Eye, 5 Degrees, Barbless, A Kirbed Forged Black Nickel #2 - 8

NEW! In 2003 **TARGUS** *Fish with the best*

TYING TRAILING SHUCKS

About 30 years ago Doug Swisher and Carl Richards, in their book, *Selective Trout*, discussed a new phenomenon in fly tying pertaining to the hatching of the mayfly, the stillborn dun. This phase has the dun partially stuck in its shuck and a portion almost fully developed. This phenomenon is now referred to as "stuck in the shuck." From this countless imitations have been developed which incorporate some form of a trailing shuck. The following will give you more options.

Marabou

Take a few fibers of marabou from the stem. Trim the butt section so that it's clean and easier to work with. Tie it on top of the hook shank. It's OK if the fibers encircle the hook shank as this will provide additional movement to the fly. Adding Ice Dubbing or Z-lon also works nicely.

Ostrich Tip

Cut off the tip of an ostrich herl and tie it on top of the hook shank so that it lays flat (not like the example). You can also add Ice Dubbing, Z-lon, or even some marabou.

Ice Dubbing

Pull some of the fibers from the package and twist them so that the fibers hang together better. Cut one end so it's easier to tie in. Then tie it on top of the hook shank. You can also intermix different colors of dubbing to achieve the colors that you want. I like the dubbing with UV in it for shucks, and just about everything else for that matter. So that you will not have a bluntly cut end, trim the dubbing at an angle so that it's thicker closer to the hook and thinner at the tip.

Z-lon

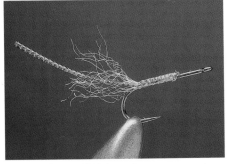

Cut a piece of Z-lon about one or two inches long. From this rope, separate out about a 1/4 to an 1/8th of it, then twist it so that the fibers hang together. Cut one end, then tie it in on top of the hook shank. So that you do not have a bluntly cut end, trim the shuck at an angle so that it is thicker closer to the hook and sparser at the tip.

Dubbing

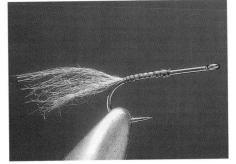

You can use virtually any type of dubbing for a trailing shuck as long as it is long fibered. This includes: Superfine Dubbing, Antron, Ice Dubbing, Z-lon, Wing N' Flash, Flashabou Dubbing, Angora, and mallard flank feathers. Shown is Superfine dubbing. Pull some fibers from the package, tie them in and trim to shape.

Emu

Take an emu feather and pull one of the fibers off the stem. Tie it in so that it lays flat on top of the hook shank. Add some Ice Dubbing or Z-lon. The emu may look like ostrich but it is much smaller and isn't quite as durable.

Hackle Tips

For those who only use natural materials in their tying, this type of shuck will be welcome. Just pluck a feather of your choice and cut out the tip by cutting the stem. Tie it onto the hook shank so that it lays flat. You can also add Z-lon or Ice Dubbing or even some marabou.

Hairline's Trailing Shucks

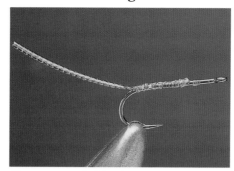

These are probably the most exact imitations of a trailing shuck. They come premade so all you have to do is take one from the package and tie it onto the hook. The clear can be made any color you wish with a simple stroke of the Chartpak marker. They come in three sizes: small, medium and large.

Trimmed Hackle

Pick a feather the color of your choice—usually brown, gray, pale yellow, orange, or grizzly—and trim the barbules with your scissors close to the stem. Tie it in so that it lays flat on the hook shank. Ice Dubbing, Z-lon, or marabou can also be added on top of this.

Reverse Hackle

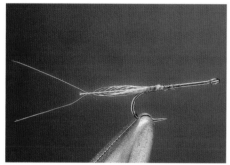

Take a feather and hold it by the tip with one of your hands. Take your other hand and pull the loose fibers against the grain of the feather. While still holding it or after some glue has been added to it, tie it on top of the hook shank. Then cut out the center of the tip so that a few fibers remain.

Ice Dubbing with Marabou

Pull some Ice Dubbing from the package and twist it to hold all the fibers together. Trim the twisted end so that it is even and then tie it in. On the top of this, tie in a small amount of marabou. The marabou should be about half way into the Ice Dubbing. If it is too long, pinch off the excess.

Ice Dubbing and Ostrich

Take some Ice Dubbing from the package and tie it on top of the hook shank. At the bend of the hook, tie in a ostrich herl and take a couple of wraps with it. It helps to select long-fibered ostrich for this so that the fibers extend back onto the dubbing when it becomes wet.

Ice Dubbing and Mallard Flank

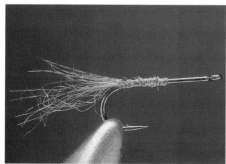

Take some Ice Dubbing from the package and tie it in on top of the hook shank. Pull some mallard fibers from their stem and tie them in on top of the dubbing. You will want the mallard to be shorter than the dubbing though.

Z-lon and Deer Hair

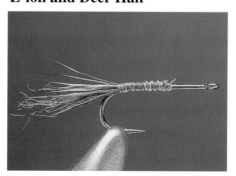

Take a few fibers from a rope of Z-lon and twist them together. This helps in working with the material. Take a few fibers of deer or elk hair and lay it on top. It is not necessary to stack the hair because the uneven ends add to the character of the shuck.

Z-lon and CDC

Tie in a few fibers of Z-lon and then add some CDC fibers over the top.

Z-lon and Coq de Leon

Separate out some Z-lon and tie it down on top of the hook shank. Pull some fibers of the coq de Leon off of the stem and tie it on top of the Z-lon. These fibers are very mottled and fairly stiff, making them great for emergers which you will want to float on or near the surface. You can also use Ice Dubbing in replacement of the Z-lon.

Reversed Hackle and Z-lon

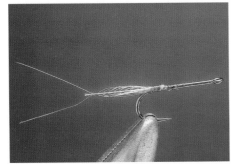

Take a few fibers of Z-lon and tie it onto the hook shank. Add the hackle shuck over this. The reverse can also be done with the hackle being tied in first and then the Z-lon added. Ice Dubbing or marabou can be substituted for the Z-lon and CDC can be used for the hackle.

Shuck and Z-lon Legs

Tie a shuck on top of the hook shank so that it lays flat. Tie some Z-lon on top of the shuck to about the middle of the shuck. To make it more realistic, pull a few Z-lon fibers out to the sides of the fly and figure-eight around them. This will make them look like the legs of the natural shuck.

Dubbing and Krystal Hair

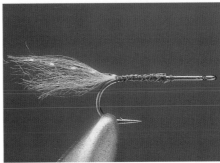

Choose whichever dubbing or fibered material you want for the main shuck and tie it on top of the hook shank (Superfine dubbing is shown). Then tie in one or two strands of Krystal Hair on top of this to add some sparkle to your shuck.

Split Tail and Z-lon

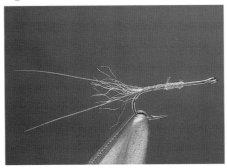

Tie in a pair of mayfly tails and separate them with a figure-eight, just like you would for an adult pattern. Over this add a few fibers of Z-lon and cut it short of the end of the split tail. Ice Dubbing or marabou are alternatives.

Ice Dubbing and Deer Legs

Take some dubbing from the package and tie it in on top of the hook shank. Then take some deer or elk hair and tie it in on top of the dubbing so that it is shorter than the dubbing. Pull a few fibers of deer hair to the sides and figure-eight around them so that they look like legs sticking out the side.

Hairline's Trailing Shucks with Z-lon

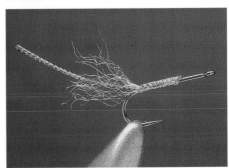

Take a trailing shuck from the package and tie it onto the top of the hook shank so that it lays flat. Add some Z-lon on top of this. The Z-lon can also be substituted with Ice Dubbing or marabou for something different.

Crippled Tail and Z-lon

Take three mayfly tails and crimp them in a pair of hemostats. Tie them on top of the hook shank and separate them with a series of figure-eights. Then tie in some Z-lon so that it encircles the tail or lays on top of it. Cut the Z-lon short of the end of the split tails. Ice Dubbing and marabou can also be used.

TYING EXTENDED BODIES

Some of the most beautiful flies incorporate an extended body. Although they are very successful in catching fish, they do take a fair amount of time to make. For those who like these type of flies however, the following will give you more options in this endeavor.

Clear Needle

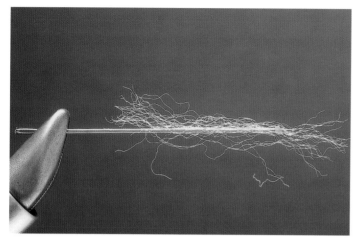

Step 1: Place a straight needle in the vise and go over it with some dubbing wax. Place a small amount of Z-lon over it.

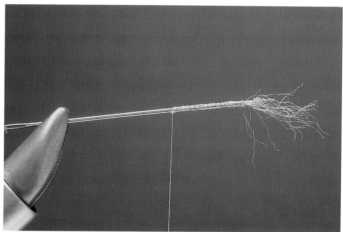

Step 2: From the point of the needle, start your thread and wrap backwards until you get the body length you want.

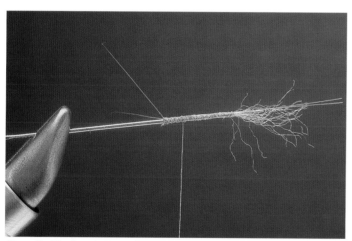

Step 3: Tie in two mayfly tails and separate them so that they remain separated just like you would for an adult pattern. Do not trim the excess tail material.

Step 4: Cut a strip of Zing Wing and tie it in at the back of the tail. Bring the thread forward and form a tapered underbody.

Step 5: Place some Zap-a-Gap on the thread body and then wrap the Zing Wing over it and tie off.

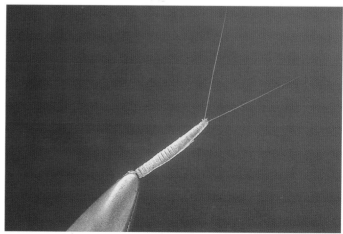

Step 6: Pull the body from the needle. To add segmentation to it and flatten it out a little bit, take a pair of hemostats and squeeze the body.

Dubbing and Needle

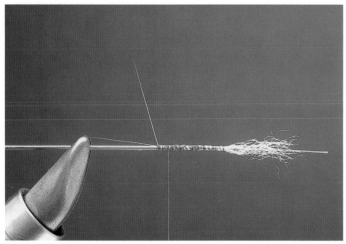

Step 1: Place some dubbing wax on the needle and put some Z-lon over it. Tie in two mayfly tails and separate them so that they remain divided.

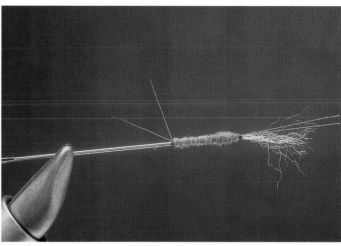

Step 2: Take the thread to the front of the needle and put some Zap-a-Gap over the thread. Add some dubbing to the needle in order to form a tapered body.

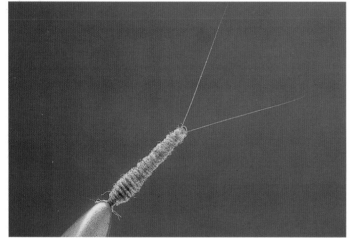

Step 3: Pull it from the needle and, if you wish, squeeze it with the hemostats.

Drake Body

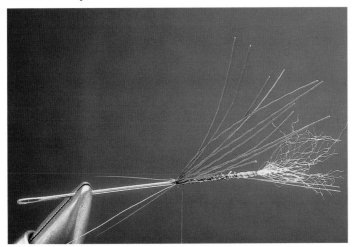

Step 1: Put some dubbing wax on the needle and then lay some Z-lon over it. Tie in two mayfly tails and separate them. Where the tail is tied in, tie in some deer hair and thread for some ribbing.

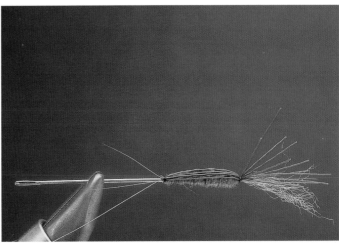

Step 2: Take the main thread to the front of the needle. Put some Zap-a-Gap over the thread body and dub a tapered body. Pull the deer hair over the top and tie down.

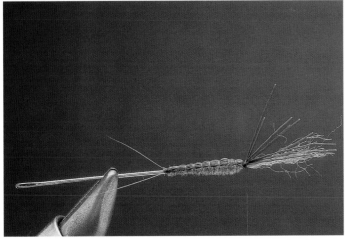

Step 3: Take the extra thread and rib the body. To make it more durable, put some glue over the body before you take it off the needle.

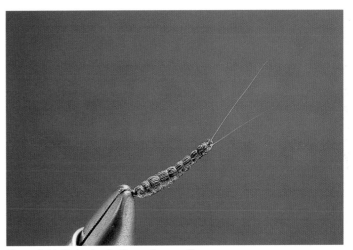

Step 4: Pull the body from the needle.

No-Thread Dubbed Body

Step 1: Put some dubbing wax on the needle and then pull some dubbing (Superfine dubbing shown) and lay it on the needle.

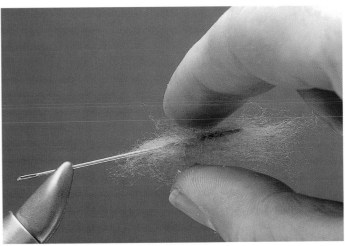

Step 2: Put some Softex on you fingers.

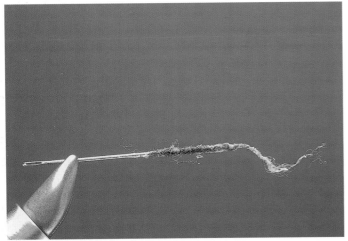

Step 3: Pinch and twist the dubbing around the needle until the body is tight. Allow it to dry, this doesn't take very long.

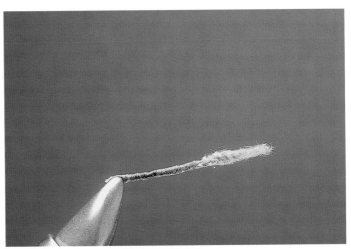

Step 4: Pull the body from the needle.

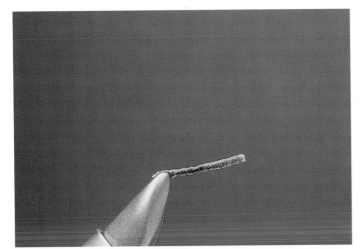

Step 5: Cut one end of the body, exposing a hole in the body which was left from the needle.

Step 6: Stick two mayfly tails into this hole and crimp the body with hemostats. Place a drop of glue at the tip of the body and where the tails are sticking out.

TYING TIPS

Working With Tubing

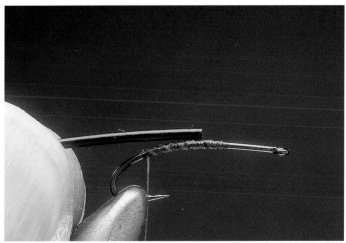

Step 1: Take the tubing in your left hand and hold it close to the tip.

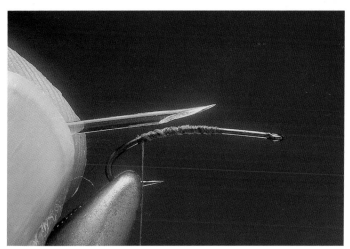

Step 2: Cut the tubing at an angle before you tie it in. This will ensure that you have a nice smooth tie-in point and not one with a little bump.

D-Rib

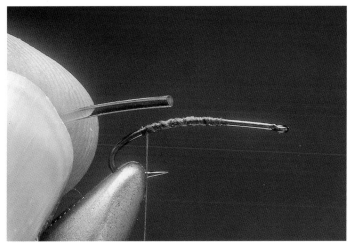

Step 1: Take the D-Rib and grab it with your left hand close to the tip.

Step 2: Cut the D-Rib at an angle before you tie it in. It is easier if you cut it starting on the flat side.

Precise Dubbing

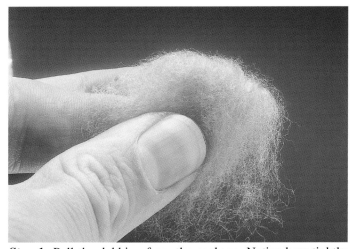

Step 1: Pull the dubbing from the package. Notice how tightly packed together the dubbing is.

Step 2: With your hand, pull the dubbing clump apart. When you do this the ends that were pulled apart will be more frayed and sparse. This is what you want.

Step 3: From this sparse end, pull out another sparse amount of dubbing. It is this portion you will dub with. By doing this twice, you are more likely to use the correct amount of dubbing. You don't want to use too much of it at one time.

WORKING WITH BIOTS FOR BODIES

Smooth Body

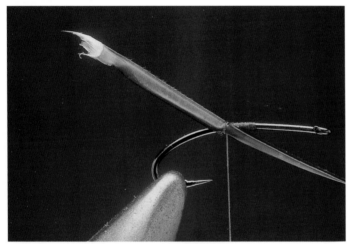

Step 1: For a smooth body, tie in the biot by the tip so that the notch at the base of the feather is facing backwards or to your left.

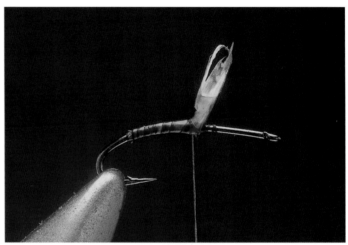

Step 2: When the biot is wrapped forward notice the nice segmentation that you get with the goose biot.

Step 3: Now notice how the segments are more transparent or non-existent when the turkey is used in the same way. For smaller flies, size 16 and under, goose biot is better for the smooth body because of its pronounced segmentation.

Ribbed Body

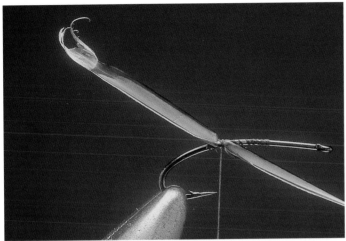

Step 1: For a ribbed body, tie in the biot by the tip so that the notch at the base of the feather is facing forward or to your right.

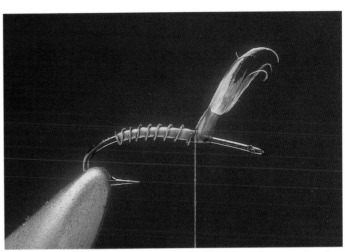

Step 2: When the goose biot is wrapped forward notice the tiny hair ribbing that is produced.

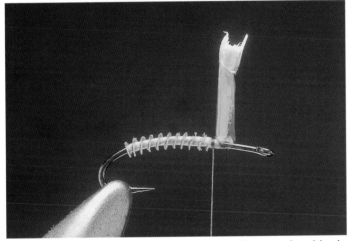

Step 3: Now notice the same tiny hair rib when a turkey biot is used. Not much difference. So if you want a hairy rib for your body, it doesn't matter if you use goose or turkey biots.

WORKING WITH MEDALLION SHEETING AND ZING WING

Wings

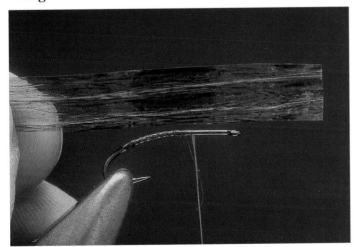

Step 1: Cut (do not tear) the sheeting to the width of your wings. Roughly an inch will do for most of the flies that you tie.

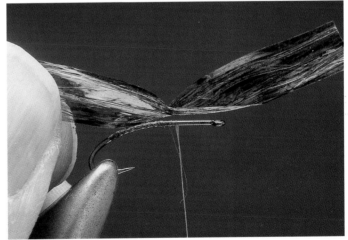

Step 2: Grab the middle of the strip and twist it. This will give you a nice tie-in point when you are ready to tie in the wings.

Step 3: To tie this wing in, use a series of figure-eights to tie it down close to the hook's eye. Once it is tied in, it will look spent or like a spinner wing.

Step 4: The wings can then be pulled back one at a time (as shown) and tied down, or both can be tied down at the same time. As you tie them down it helps if you pull back and kind of pinch the wing against the hook so that it does not twist or kink up.

For emergers, the wings are pulled back and lie along the sides of the fly. For adult patterns, the wings are pulled straight back and on top of the hook.

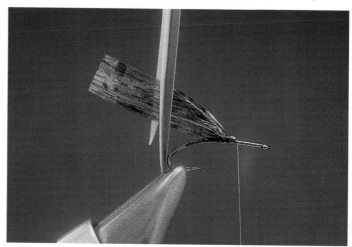

Step 5: To trim the wings into the shape of an adult mayfly, pull the wings back at an angle, come over the top of them and cut. Hold the scissors straight up and down as you make the cut. Then just round off the edges.

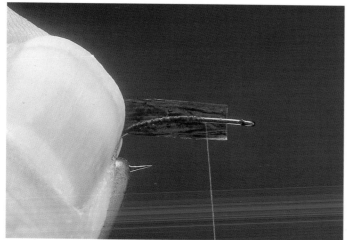

Step 6: When using this material for a wing case, or any solid type of material, it helps if you first hold the material along the side of the fly towards you.

Then as you take your thread around it and the hook, the material will form around the hook more evenly and you will be less likely to have material off to one side or the other.

Divided Mayfly Tails

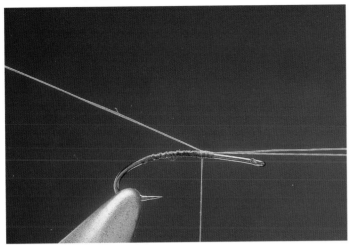

Step 1: Starting in the thorax area, tie in the amount of tail fibers you want.

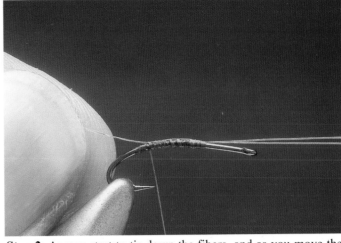

Step 2: As you start to tie down the fibers, and as you move the thread from the front towards the back, pull up and back on the fibers with your free hand. This will keep the fibers on top of the hook shank and not let them roll off to one side.

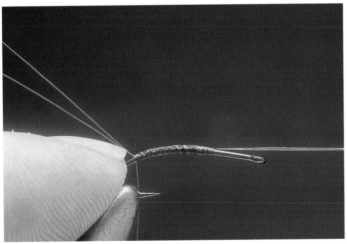

Step 3: With your tails now in place, take your index finger and push up into the fibers so that they separate. This can also be done by just sweeping your finger up and through the fibers.

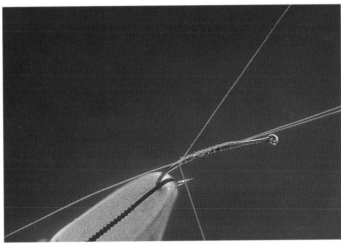

Step 4: Once they are separated, pull the fibers to each side of the hook. To begin the figure-eight, first start by winding the thread from the underside and coming up between the fibers on the side towards you. Then take one turn of thread just in front of the tails.

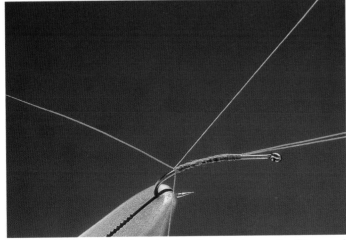

Step 5: Take a turn of thread going down between the fibers and away from you (while the thread is pushing up against the far tail.) Then bring the thread up to the hook and take a turn of thread. If the tails are bent down, take a turn of thread around the underside of the tails to help lift them up.

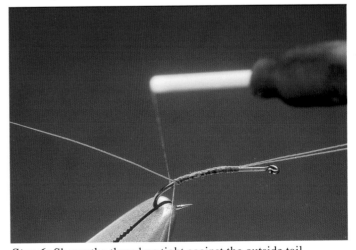

Step 6: Shows the thread up tight against the outside tail.

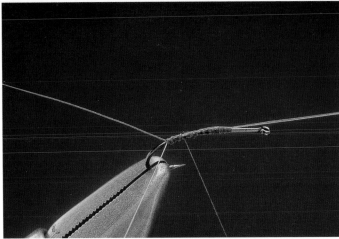

Step 7: Take one turn of thread under the tail to lift it and you are done.

Marabou Bodies

Step 1: Pull or cut off several fibers from the stem.

Step 2: Grab the fibers close to the tips and then tie them in.

Step 3: Once they are tied in, twist the fibers together creating a marabou rope. This will make the fibers stick out more from the stem and therefore be less likely to get tied down. Since the fibers are twisted together, different colors of marabou can be used if you wish.

Step 4: Next you are ready to wrap it forward.

Partridge Legs

Step 1: Select a well-preserved feather with no broken fibers.

Step 2: Cut the tip out of the feather creating a "V" in it. The "V" will separate into two equal groups when you press your fingernail down into it once the feather is tied in. This makes having an equal number of fibers on each side of your fly a lot easier.

Flat Soft-Hackle Legs

Step 1: Wrap a hen neck feather forward just like you would any hackle.

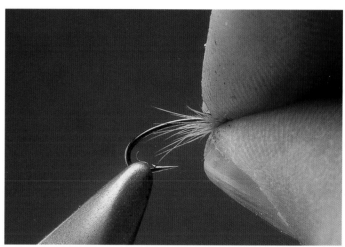

Step 2: To make it flat without cutting out any of the fibers, simply take your fingers and pinch the hackle against the hook.

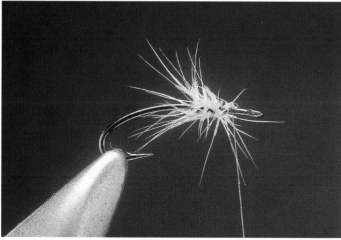

Step 3: This will leave the fibers sticking out the sides of the fly, letting it ride flush on the surface.

Step 4: Front view of the smashed-down soft hackle.

ADULT MAYFLY COLOR CHART

Blue-Winged Olive

Light Olive

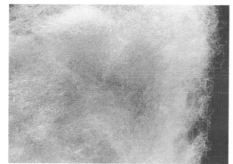

Medium Olive

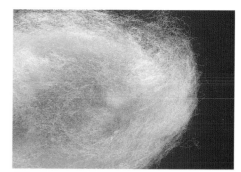

Gray/Olive

Pale Morning Dun

Olive/Yellow

Yellow/Olive

Light Olive

Baetis

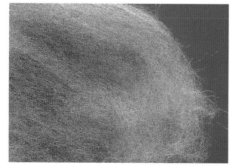

Gray Dun

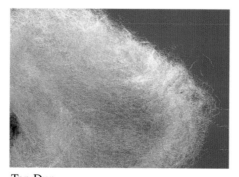

Tan Dun

Olive Dun

Callibaetis

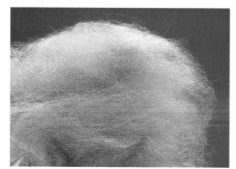

Olive/Tan

Gray

Tan

Sulphur

Orange

Yellow

Trico

Gray/Black

Brown/Black

Mahogany Dun

Red Quill

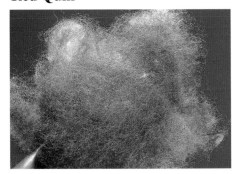

MAYFLY NYMPH COLOR CHART

Blue-Winged Olive

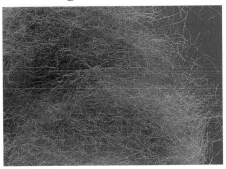

Olive

Dark Olive

Olive/Brown

Brown/Olive

Pale Morning Dun

Medium Brown

Dark Brown

Brown/Olive

Rusty/Brown

Callibaetis

Tan

Medium Tan

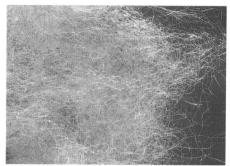

Tan/Olive

Red Quill

Dark Brown

Sulphur

Dark Brown

Mahogany Dun

Dark Brown

Trico

Dark Gray/Black/Brown

Chapter 2

NYMPHS

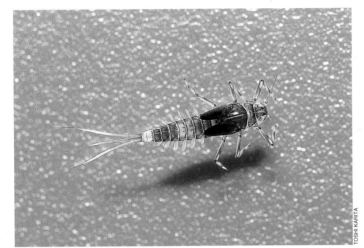

Biot Nymph

Hook:	Targus 200, or equivalent, size 14-22
Tail:	Partridge
Thread:	Match the body color
Body:	Turkey or Hareline's Premo goose biots
Wing Case:	Medallion sheeting or Flashback
Thorax:	Small flies, micro dry-fly dubbing; larger flies, Awesome Possum dubbing
Legs:	Partridge
Head:	Bead head optional

When it comes to Colorado, fly fishing and *Baetis* go hand in hand. For many, *Baetis* means one thing, Blue-Winged Olives. Although this is true, *Baetis* here means any small swimming mayfly that you might encounter. These flies are easy to identify because they are small, slender, and have small gills alongside their body. With that said, it is no wonder the Biot Nymph works so well.

The Biot Nymph is made of just what its name implies, biots. The biot is tied in by the tip and wrapped forward so you get a fuzzy rib. This fuzzy rib represent the segmented body and also the tiny gills that line the body. As the biot is wrapped forward, a natural taper is built into the body that only goose biot can create. The goose biot is a solid feather and is somewhat thicker than the turkey biot. On larger sizes, such 16 and bigger, the turkey biot is best because of its length.

In the picture of the natural, you can see how slender and small the *Baetis* really is. The artificial has much the same characteristics when you view them side by side. The *Baetis* tail is not a solid color and that is why partridge is used. The body is slim and has gills so goose biot is perfect for this body part. The wing case is dark and has a sheen to it, so, Medallion sheeting is used to represent these characteristics. The legs are not a solid color so partridge is once again used.

The nice thing about this fly is that it is so easy to tie. Just because a fly is easy to tie, however, does not mean that it doesn't work. This fly has accounted for numerous fish on waters such as the South Platte and the Frying Pan, so you can count on it working wherever you fish.

Even though this fly is meant to be fished on the bottom like most nymphs, do not hold yourself to fishing this one method. Grease it up and fish it in the surface film for a floating nymph. This is best done when it is trailed behind a more buoyant fly so that strikes can be detected. Also, try tying a few up on a curved hook. Just changing the hook style can mean the difference between success and failure.

The Biot Nymph has been described as a fly for the Blue-Winged Olive but try it for other insects as well. Another insect that lends itself nicely to this fly is the Pale Morning Dun. Instead of using olive body parts, change the color to a medium or dark brown and tan for a *Callibaetis*.

Step 1: Tie in some partridge fibers for the tail. Tie in the biot by the tip so that the notch is facing forward. Leave the tail's excess material in place until the biot is wrapped over it. This will leave you with a smooth underbody.

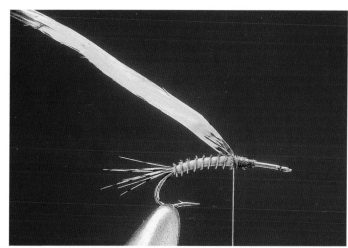

Step 2: Wrap the biot forward until you are about a 1/3 back from the hook eye, then tie in the sheeting for the wing case.

Step 3: Dub the thorax but leave enough room for the legs and the wing case to be tied down.

Step 4: Cut a "V" in a partridge feather and tie it in so that the tips extend back just beyond the wing case.

Step 5: Pull the wing case over the top and make sure you have an equal number of partgidge fibers sticking out each side.

Finished fly.

Biot Nymph Brown

Hook:	Targus 200, or equivalent, size 14-22
Tail:	Partridge
Thread:	Brown
Body:	Turkey or Hareline's Premo goose biots brown
Wing Case:	Medallion sheeting brown or Flashback brown
Thorax:	Small flies, micro dry-fly dubbing; larger flies, brown Awesome Possum dubbing
Legs:	Partridge

Tan Biot Nymph

Hook:	Targus 200, or equivalent, size 14-22
Tail:	Partridge
Thread:	Tan
Body:	Turkey or Hareline's Premo goose biots tan
Wing Case:	Medallion sheeting tan or Flashback tan
Thorax:	Small flies, micro dry-fly dubbing; larger flies, tan Awesome Possum dubbing
Legs:	Partridge

Gray Biot Nymph

Hook:	Targus 200, or equivalent, size 14-22
Thread:	Gray
Body:	Turkey or Hareline's Premo goose biots gray
Wing Case:	Medallion sheeting medium dun or Flashback gray
Thorax:	Small flies, micro dry-fly dubbing; larger flies, gray Awesome Possum
Legs:	Partridge

Trico Nymph

Hook:	Targus 200, or equivalent, size 18-22
Thread:	Black
Tail:	Partridge
Body:	Turkey biot
Gills:	Emu
Shellback:	Medallion sheeting dark dun
Thorax:	Micro dry-fly dubbing Trico color
Legs:	Partridge

The Trico Nymph is tied in much the same way as the Biot Nymph with a few alterations. First, the tail should be tied a little longer than normal, plus the Trico's body is short and robust for its size. Kind of a muscle man of the small nymphs. Before the biot is wrapped forward, you must first make a tapered underbody. This is done by wrapping the thread up and down the hook shank until a nice, evenly-tapered body is formed. The body is not quite as long as the Biot Nymph. The biot should be wrapped just beyond the halfway mark, leaving enough room for a thicker-than-normal thorax. Then just in front of the wing case, before the thorax is formed, tie in a couple of emu feather tips for the gills.

Most anglers think of the Trico as a small black fly (18-22), which they are, but brown can be equally as effective. Depending on which species is in your home waters, the brown Trico Nymph just might outperform the black one.

One of the most effective ways to fish this little nymph is during the spinner fall. When these things hatch, they really hatch. Clouds of Tricos hover over the water and the not-so-lucky ones blanket the water's surface. With so many spinners on the water, how are trout going to pick your offering? Try floating a Trico Nymph. On the Colorado River, and the section of the South Platte known as the Dream Stream, this presentation can be deadly.

Step 1: Tie in some partridge fibers for the tail so that they are roughly the length of the hook gap.

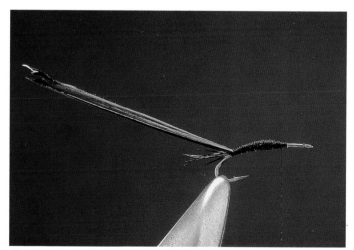

Step 2: Tie in the biot by the tip so that the notch is facing forward. Form an underbody with your thread so that it tapers from the back to the front.

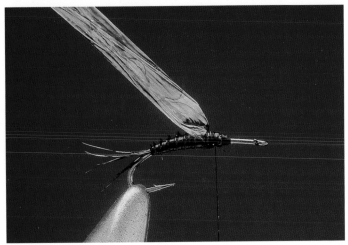

Step 3: Wrap the biot forward so that the body is about 1/3 back from the hook eye. Tie in the wing case.

Step 4: Take two emu fibers and tie them in so that the tips extend back to the middle of the body on the side away from you. Do the same thing on the side towards you. This is done right in front of the wing case.

Step 5: Dub the thorax full.

Step 6: Tie in some partridge for the legs by cutting a "V" in the feather so that they extend back just beyond the wing case. Pull the wing case over the top and tie off.

Finished fly.

TOSHI KARITA

Baetis Nymph

Hook:	Targus 200, or equivalent, size 14-22
Thread:	Match the body color
Tail:	Partridge
Body:	Small D-Rib
Wing Case:	Medallion sheeting
Legs:	Partridge
Thorax:	Micro dry-fly dubbing for small flies; Awesome Possum dubbing for larger flies
Head:	Bead head optional

Of all the small mayfly nymphs I have tied over the years, this one has become my go-to fly. Just like its cousin the Biot Nymph, its slender body fits into the *Baetis* family quite nicely. The *Baetis* family includes Blue-Winged Olives, Pale Morning Duns, and *Callibaetis*. Unlike the Biot Nymph, this fly uses new materials for the body. The first is micro tubing. Micro tubing is a small, hollow tubing that can be stretched down to tie size 24s. Before it is tied in, cut the tubing at an angle so there is minimal build up. The first several wraps should be made with the tubing under a lot of tension. As you progress up the hook shank, relax the tension a little, until you get up to a stopping point where you do not want any tension at all. This will create a tapered body which is translucent and segmented. You can also place a piece of FisHair in the tubing before wrapping it to give the body even more segmentation or wrap it between the segmentations.

D-Rib is also a new material; it's a translucent material but unlike tubing which is hollow, it's in the shape of a "D." This shape gives the tier very definite humplike segmentations as opposed to tubing which lies flat. Just like with tubing, you'll want to cut the material at an angle before you tie it in. A little trick that can be used with both materials after the body has been wrapped is to take a Magic Marker and run it over the top of it. The top of the material will take the color of the marker, and some of the color will soak down inbetween the wraps. This gives your fly a two-tone appearance.

Another component of the Baetis nymph that is somewhat different from the norm is how the wing case is tied in. On most flies, the wing case is tied in before the thorax is formed and then pulled over the top. On this fly, the wing case is tied in at the hook eye, extending out over it. By doing it this way, the legs can be tied in the middle of the thorax making it look more natural. When the wing case is pulled back, the legs will splay out into two equal groups and sweep backwards. By doing just this one step a little differently, you are a step closer to a more anatomically correct fly. After all, how many bugs have legs sticking out of their heads?

Step 1: Tie in a few fibers of partridge for the tail.

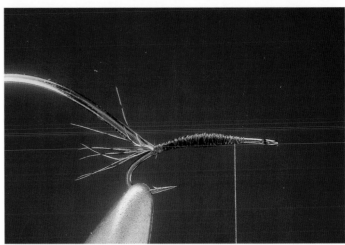

Step 2: Cut the D-Rib at an angle and tie it in by the tip so that when you wrap it forward the semi curved side is on top.

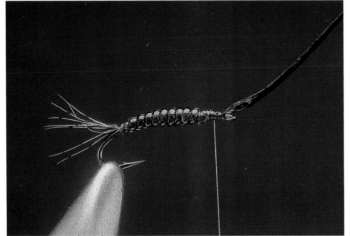

Step 3: Wrap the D-Rib forward over a tapered underbody of thread. Start by stretching the material all the way and as you go up the hook shank ease up on the tension. You should end about a 1/4 of the way back from the hook eye. Then tie in a piece of the sheeting for the wing case so that it goes out over the hook eye.

Step 4: Take a partridge feather and cut a "V" in it. Tie it in with the tips sticking out over the hook eye in the middle of the thorax.

Step 5: Cut off the excess partridge and cover it with the dubbing. Place some dubbing in front of the partridge so that the feather stands up or slightly backwards. When you are done with the dubbing you'll want the thread to end up at the back of the thorax. The partridge should be standing straight up and slightly backwards.

Step 6: From the hook eye going back, take your index fingernail and push down on the partridge so that it separates into two equal groups. With the partridge divided, pull the wing case over the top and tie it down in the back of the thorax. Pull the thread under the body up to the eye and tie off.

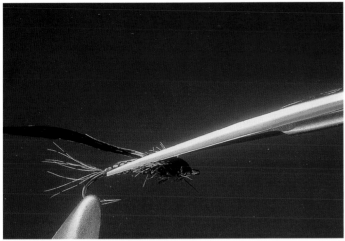 

Step 7: Take your left hand and grab the excess wing case and pull it straight back. While it's under tension cut it short with your scissors at an angle. This will create a "V" in the wing case.

Finished Baetis Nymph (side view).

Baetis Nymph, Brown

Hook:	Targus 200, or equivalent, size 14-22
Thread:	Brown
Tail:	Partridge
Body:	Micro tubing or small D-Rib, brown
Wing Case:	Medallion sheeting, brown or Flashback brown
Thorax:	Small flies, micro dry-fly dubbing; larger flies brown Awesome Possum
Legs:	Partridge

Baetis Nymph, Tan

Hook:	Targus 200, or equivalent, size 14-22
Thread:	Tan
Tail:	Partridge
Body:	Micro tubing or small D-Rib tan
Wing Case:	Medallion sheeting, tan, or tan Flashback
Thorax:	Small flies, micro dry-fly dubbing; larger flies, tan Awesome Possum
Legs:	Partridge

Baetis Nymph, Black

Hook:	Targus 200, or equivalent, size 14-22
Thread:	Black
Tail:	Partridge
Body:	Micro tubing or small D-Rib, black
Wing Case:	Medallion sheeting dark dun or Flashback dark dun or black
Thorax:	Small flies, micro dry-fly dubbing; larger flies, black Awesome Possum

TOSHI KARITA

Gilled Nymph

Hook:	Targus 200/, or equivalent, size 10-18
Tail:	Ostrich tips
Body:	Ostrich herl
Ribbing:	Fine wire or ultra wire
Wing Case:	Medallion sheeting
Thorax:	Awesome Possum dubbing or squirrel
Legs:	Partridge
Head:	Bead head optional

When it comes to fishing lakes, anglers pretty much have one choice for a mayfly imitation, the *Callibaetis*. This insect is very widespread and should not be overlooked by lake fishermen. Unlike mayflies, which inhabit moving waters and get their oxygen from this flow, the *Callibaetis* must move around and flap its gills to extract oxygen. Why is this important to know? Well, as mentioned before, if you do not know what the bug looks like or, even more importantly, how it acts and moves in the water, how can you expect to imitate it?

Since the *Callibaetis* is a swimmer and has fairly large, pulsating gills, pick your materials for the body accordingly. The choice for this fly is ostrich. It's soft and fibrous, so when it is moved through the water will pulsate. This gives the illusion of gills and can't be refused by hungry trout. Even though ostrich has been used in much the same manner on other flies, the Gilled Nymph takes it one step further. Once the body has been wrapped, a wire ribbing is used to reinforce this fragile material and give it some segmentation. Then a bodkin is heated up and laid on top of it. This will singe the ostrich down below the wire, exposing the ribbing. Plus, it gives your fly a flat and clean-looking appearance. Using ostrich for the body means that more than one feather can and will be used. For example, when I am tying a *Callibaetis* fly, the body is composed of two tan and one olive ostrich herl. This way the body will have just a hint of olive with

the overall color being tan. I also like to use two olive and one tan for the *Callibaetis*. This color combination is used primarily in the summer when the fauna has turned from drab brown to colorful green, in most instances. It's important to keep in mind that for camouflage the aquatic life (insects) will take on the colors of their environment. For the most part, spring and fall insects will have more brown and the summer insects will have more greens and olives. Besides a great *Callibaetis* imitation, another heavily-gilled critter lends itself nicely to this pattern, the Green Drake nymph. I like to use olive, brown and gray ostrich twisted together to make the body a dirty olive/brown color. Since this version will be tied on larger hooks, before you wrap the body forward first place some dubbing down to add bulk to the body.

The Gilled Nymph has been primarily described as a *Callibaetis* nymph and with good reason. It has accounted for more fish in still waters than just about any other fly that I fish. Regardless of whether the fly is fished alone while I stalk a lone fish or it's trailed behind some other fly as a searching pattern. However, it should not be overlooked for other techniques. While fishing the Gunnison River with Charlie Gillman one summer, a brown-gilled nymph trailed behind a high-floating dry proved to be the most effective fly of the trip. In the size range 14-16 (the size I use most often), the movement of this fly in the water is hard to beat.

Step 1: Take three ostrich herls and even up their tips. Tie them in so that the tips extend out for a tail. Tie in some wire for the ribbing.

Step 2: Twist the herl together into a single rope. On larger flies such as the green drakes, it helps if you first dub a tapered underbody to make it more full.

Step 3: Wrap the ostrich forward.

Step 4: Wrap the ribbing forward and take care not to to tie down any of the ostrich feathers.

Step 5: Cut the ostrich flat on top of the fly and the bottom.

Step 6: Take your bodkin and heat it up. Then lay it on top of the body so that the ostrich is singed down to the wire rib. On drake patterns this should also be done on the bottom. On smaller flies it doesn't matter.

Step 7: Tie in the wing case and dub the thorax.

Step 8: Tie in the partridge for the legs so that they extend back just beyond the wing case.

Step 9: Pull the wing case over the top and make sure that you have equal numbers of fibers on each side of the thorax and tie off.

Finished Gilled Nymph (side view).

Gilled Nymph, Olive

Hook:	Targus 200/, or equivalent, size 10-18
Thread:	Olive
Tail:	Ostrich tips, olive
Ribbing:	Fine wire or ultra wire
Body:	Ostrich herl, olive
Wing Case:	Medallion sheeting medium dun or Flashback olive
Thorax:	Awesome Possum or squirrel, olive
Legs:	Partridge

Gilled Nymph, Brown

Hook:	Targus 200/, or equivalent, size 10-14
Thread:	Brown
Tail:	Ostrich tips, brown
Ribbing:	Fine wire or ultra wire
Body:	Ostrich herl brown
Wing Case:	Medallion sheeting brown or Flashback brown
Thorax:	Awesome Possum or squirrel, brown
Legs:	Partridge

Gilled Nymph, Gray

Hook:	Targus 200/, or equivalent, size 10-14
Thread:	Gray
Tail:	Ostrich tips, gray
Ribbing:	Fine wire or ultra wire
Body:	Ostrich herl, gray
Wing Case:	Medallion sheeting medium dun or Flashback gray
Thorax:	Awesome Possum or Flashback gray
Legs:	Partridge

TOSHI KARITA

Marabou Nymph

Hook:	Targus 200, or equivalent, size 10-18
Thread:	Match the body color
Tail:	Marabou
Ribbing:	Fine wire or ultra wire
Body:	Marabou
Shellback:	Medallion sheeting
Thorax:	Marabou
Legs:	Partridge
Head:	Bead head optional

Marabou Nymphs also have a lot of movement built into them. The Gilled Nymph used ostrich for movement, and the Marabou in this pattern has the same qualities. It is soft and flows freely in the water. But, unlike the ostrich, its fibers are longer and not quite as pronounced.

Tie the marabou in by its tips, then twisted it into a rope. As you do this, the fibers of the feather spiral outwards, making them stand out. All you have to do then is wrap the rope forward and rib it for durability. The top and bottom can be trimmed, if you wish, so that the fibers stick out just on the sides of the abdomen. When I am rushed for time (like the night before a trip) and need a gilled nymph, this fly is the one that gets tied up. Again, since the marabou is twisted together, various colors can be used making it ideal for the Green Drake.

The problem with using marabou in this fashion is that when it gets wet, it tends to plaster against the body and not reveal its fibers like the ostrich does. Even though this particular characteristic is absent, a new look is achieved. The matted-down fibers along the body give almost a halo face to the abdomen. This looks like the gills being laid back on a natural. This is even more pronounced when you use light and dark fibers intertwined in the rope.

Instead of using dubbing for the thorax like the Gilled Nymph, marabou is once again used. The result is a fly made entirely of marabou with all kinds of movement. In order for the marabou to come to life, though, do not rely only on the current. Twitch the rod tip occasionally so that the fibers are freed and become more noticeable to the fish. As the fly regains its momentum within the current, the marabou will once again flatten against the sides. The combination of these movements will give the marabou a breathing motion.

Using the rod to create movement in the body brings the whole fly into motion, making it look more natural. Remember, do not rely solely on the fly to do all the work, it take the combination of the angler and materials used to get the most out of your fly. The colors I use most are usually earth tones: olives, grays, and browns. Olives and grays are used for *Baetis* and the brown shades are used for Pale Morning Duns. More times than not, a size-16 fly will find its way onto the end of my line. Occasionally, a 14 will appear. This fly is outstanding when tied with a bead head, which provides even more movement.

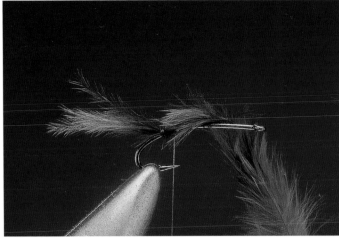

Step 1: Cut off some fibers of marabou and tie the tips in so that they extend out the back of the fly. This will only require a wrap or two of thread. Then tie in the wire for the ribbing. Take the thread up to the thorax area which is about 1/3 back from the hook eye.

Step 2: Twist the marabou into a rope with your fingers, or one single strand of material. Then wrap it forward. Twisting it makes the fibers stick straight out from the hook shank. Carefully wrap the wire through the body making sure that you do not tie down too many fibers. You can leave the body as is or you can trim it flat on the top and the bottom so just the fibers stick out the sides of the fly.

Step 3: Cut a strip of the Medallion sheeting for the wing case and tie it in where you left off with the marabou.

Step 4: Take some more marabou and tie it in by the tips in the thorax. Twist it and wrap it through the thorax. To make the thorax fuller looking when the fly gets wet, place some dubbing in the thorax first before you wrap the marabou.

Step 5: Cut a "V" in a partridge feather and tie it in so that the tips stick towards the back and extend just beyond the wing case.

Step 6: Pull the wing case over the top and tie off.

Finished Marabou Nymph.

Marabou Nymph, Tan

Hook:	Targus 200, or equivalent, size 10-16
Thread:	Tan
Tail:	Marabou, tan
Ribbing:	Fine wire or ultra wire
Body:	Marabou, tan
Wing Case:	Medallion sheeting, tan or Flashback tan
Thorax:	Marabou, tan
Legs:	Partridge

Marabou Nymph, Brown

Hook:	Targus 200, or equivalent, size 10-16
Thread:	Brown
Tail:	Marabou brown
Ribbing:	Fine wire or ultra wire
Body:	Marabou brown
Wing Case:	Medallion sheeting, brown or Flashback brown
Thorax:	Marabou, brown
Legs:	Partridge

Marabou Nymph, Black

Hook:	Targus 200, or equivalent, size 10-16.
Thread:	Black
Tail:	Marabou black
Ribbing:	Fine wire or ultra wire
Body:	Marabou black
Wing Case:	Medallion sheeting dark dun or Flashback black
Thorax:	Marabou black
Legs:	Partridge

TOSHI KARITA

Hare's Ear Special

Hook:	Targus 200, or equivalent, size 10-16
Thread:	Match body color
Tail:	Marabou
Back Strap:	Mottled turkey
Ribbing:	Fine wire or ultra wire
Body:	Hare's ear or squirrel
Wing Case:	Mottled turkey
horax:	Same as body
Legs:	Partridge
Head:	Bead head optional

All fly-fishermen have heard of the Gold Ribbed Hare's Ear. There are probably as many variations of this fly as there are fly tiers. The standard Hare's Ear is a generic fly which represents just about any aquatic insect, but it is most like the mayfly. When I think of a mayfly nymph I picture a slim, sleek little fly that is very clean looking. When you use hare's mask dubbing, this illusion doesn't materialize.

In order to make the fly a little more appealing to me, and hopefully trout, a back strap was added to the abdomen in order to make the ribbing more pronounced and sleek in appearance. Marabou or feather fluff (for a tail) and partridge (for legs) are winning materials to add to any fly, and the Hare's Ear is no exception. With just a few modifications, this fly has gained a respectful place in my fly box. In olives and tans it is a good representation of the *Callibaetis,* and browns in the smaller sizes for Pale Morning duns.

The Gold Ribbed Hare's Ear is not used for a specific hatch but is more of a searching fly. A general fly like this is great to use on unfamiliar waters, especially on a large river such as the Gunnison. The variations a tier can make on this fly are almost endless with today's array of materials. For example, try using different colored Flashback over the abdomen and thorax for a flash Hare's Ear. Tie in some of the micro round rubber for legs just for kicks. And by all means, try it with a bead head as well.

Why should a tier try tying one fly with so many different arrangements? There are so many fishermen out on the waters these days that a fish can see the same thing over and over again until they won't respond to it anymore. Or at least not as often. By changing your fly a little bit, the fish can be thrown off balance and fooled into taking your modified fly.

Step 1: Tie in the marabou so that it extends a 1/3 of the way back beyond the hook.

Step 2: Tie in the back strap, fine wire and dub the body. You should be 1/3 the way back from the hook eye.

Step 3: Pull the turkey over the back and tie it down. Then segment the body with the wire.

Step 4: Fold the turkey back for the wing case and dub the thorax.

Step 5: Cut a "V" in the partridge and tie it in for the legs. They should extend just past the wing case.

Step 6: Pull the wing case forward and tie off. You can pick out the body and thorax some more at this point to make it even more scraggly.

Finished Hare's Ear Special (top view).

Hare's Ear, Tan

Hook:	Targus 200, or equivalent, size 10-16
Thread:	Tan
Tail:	Marabou, tan
Ribbing:	Fine wire or ultra wire
Back Strap:	Mottled turkey, tan
Body:	Hare's ear or squirrel, tan
Wing Case:	Mottled turkey, tan
Thorax:	Hare's ear or squirrel, tan
Legs:	Partridge

Hare's Ear, Brown

Hook:	Targus 200, or equivalent, size 10-16
Thread:	Brown
Tail:	Marabou, brown
Ribbing:	Fine wire or ultra wire
Back Strap:	Mottled turkey, brown
Body:	Hare's ear or squirrel, brown
Wing Case:	Mottled turkey, brown
Thorax:	Hare's ear or squirrel, brown
Legs:	Partridge

Hare's Ear, Olive

Hook:	Targus 200, or equivalent, size 10-16
Thread:	Olive
Tail:	Marabou, olive
Ribbing:	Fine wire or ultra wire
Back Strap:	Mottled turkey, olive
Body:	Hare's ear or squirrel, olive
Wing Case:	Mottled turkey, olive
Thorax:	Olive hare's ear or squirrel
Legs:	Partridge

TOSHI KARITA

Quick Descent Nymph

Hook:	Targus 200, or equivalent, size 10-16
Thread:	Match color of the body
Tail:	Partridge
Body:	Quick Descent dubbing
Overbody:	Clear micro or midge tubing
Shellback:	Flashback
Legs:	Partridge
Thorax:	Quick Descent dubbing
Head:	Bead head optional

One of the hottest materials fly tiers have started using in the last several years is gold beads. Virtually every standard nymph pattern now has a bead in front of it. Their popularity has remained because quite simply they help catch fish. Is this because of the flash or is it because the fly is being fished at the depths in which it should have been fished all along? The latter is more likely and that is why this new material used in the Quick Descent fly will be sure to catch on.

The design of this fly is not unique, it has a tail, body, wing case and legs. The difference is in the dubbing. The new material is called Quick Descent dubbing and is produced by Hareline Dubbin. Your fly will sink like a rock. Most dubbings are made from natural furs or synthetics, Quick Descent dubbing is made of aluminum. It has been shaved very fine. It can be dubbed down to the finest flies that you can tie and it will not rust. Plus, when you add the ribbing of ultra wire, a fast-sinking fly is the result.

For the smallest of flies, only a few strands are needed and should be dubbed onto the thread just like any other dubbing.

You'd think that something made of metal would be hard to work with but this couldn't be further from the truth, it is very easy to use. In fact, it's as easy to put on your thread as any dubbing on the market. Also, dubbing wax is not needed.

For a fast-sinking fly, try tying this pattern with copper dubbing, brown ultra wire, and copper Flashback. The result is like a flashy Brassie and Pheasant Tail rolled into one. After the body has been dubbed and ribbed, take a pair of needlenose pliers and squeeze the body and thorax. This results in a flattened fly. Moreover, if you use the pliers right, the teeth will put a center line down the middle of the body, adding more character to the fly. What other dubbing has these kind of options? I'm sure you are already imagining just what you can create when you get to your vise.

This fly is great to use when fish are feeding in the middle of the water column. No additional weight is required, avoiding spooking the fish. For a super dredger nymph, place a bead on the hook first, before the rest of the fly is finished.

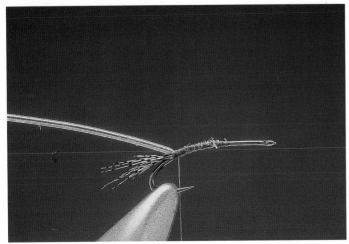

Step 1: Tie in several fibers of partridge for the tail. Cut the tubing at an angle and tie it in.

Step 2: Dub the body so that it tapers from the back to the front, about 1/4 the way back from the hook eye.

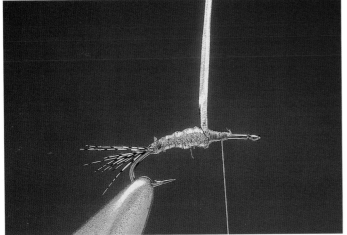

Step 3: Wrap the tubing over the body and tie in the wing case.

Step 4: Dub a full thorax and tie in some partridge for the legs. The tips of the partridge should extend back just beyond the shellback.

Step 5: Pull the wing case forward and tie off. To make the fly flat, take a pair of pliers and squeeze the body and thorax.

Finished Quick Descent Nymph (side view).

Quick Descent Nymph, Black

Hook:	Targus 200, or equivalent, size 10-16.
Thread:	Black
Tail:	Partridge
Body:	Quick Descent dubbing black
Overbody:	Micro tubing or small D-Rib
Wing Case:	Flashback, black
Thorax:	Quick Descent dubbing, black
Legs:	Partridge

Quick Descent Nymph, Brown

Hook:	Targus 200, or equivalent, size 10-16
Thread:	Brown
Tail:	Partridge
Body:	Quick Descent dubbing, brown
Over Body:	Micro tubing or small D-Rib
Wing Case:	Flashback, brown
Thorax:	Quick Descent dubbing, brown
Legs:	Partridge

Quick Descent Nymph, Olive

Hook:	Targus 200, or equivalent, size 10-16
Thread:	Olive
Tail:	Partridge
Body:	Quick Descent dubbing, olive
Over Body:	Micro tubing or small D-Rib
Wing Case:	Flashback olive
Thorax:	Quick Descent dubbing, olive
Legs:	Partridge

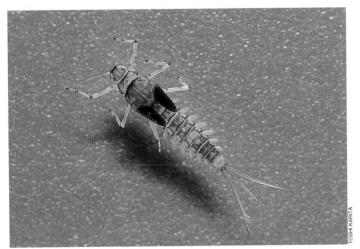

TOSHI KARITA

Gilled Pheasant Tail

Hook:	Targus 200, or equivalent, size 14-20
Thread:	Match body color
Body:	Pheasant tail fibers
Ribbing:	Micro tubing
Wing Case:	Medallion sheeting or Flashback
Thorax:	Dubbing or peacock
Legs:	Pheasant tail fibers or partridge
Head:	Bead if you wish
Gills:	Marabou

Just like the Hare's Ear, the Pheasant Tail Nymph has a long and distinguished history. It too comes in a variety of styles depending on the fly tier. This particular version falls in line with the others in that a few new materials have been added. Experimenting with new materials is what makes fly tying so much fun. Many new materials come out each year. This gives the fly tier new and exciting options, while leaving the fly shop owner reaching for the bottle of aspirin.

This is a simple mayfly pattern that will have even the novice grinning with their results. Fish the Gilled Pheasant Tail during a Blue-Winged Olive or Pale Morning Dun hatch, or use it for any small-mayfly hatch. It can also be categorized as a guide fly because of its simple design. It is sparse and narrow, and will match just about any mayfly nymph in the stream.

When tying small flies, it's important to remember to first cut the tubing or D-Rib at an angle, before you tie it in. This eliminates any hump or build-up at the tie-in point. Also, as you wrap the material forward, vary the tension to help create a tapered body. If a flat and wide-bodied fly is desired, form a tapered underbody with the heavy metal dubbing. Then after the tubing is wrapped over it, squeeze it with the pliers. Be careful not to cut the tubing. If you do use the pliers, it is best to use a pair with smooth jaws.

For the shellback, you can use whatever your heart desires: Medallion sheeting, Flashback, or pheasant tail fibers. The same holds true for the legs. Try using partridge or other soft-hackle fibers, along with pheasant tail. The colors range from the original rust to olive to black. These three colors are by far the most widely used. The rust represents the Pale Morning Dun and the others can be used for a wide variety of *Baetis* nymphs. As with so many flies today, a bead can be placed on the hook. For something new, try dubbing the thorax with the heavy metal dubbing.

Since this fly is so narrow and slender, a little bit of floatant will help it to remain in the surface film. The Gilled Pheasant Tail can be deadly when trailed behind an adult pattern. If you fish this fly in the film, use the tubing. If you are fishing it as a nymph, I suggest the D-Rib. Since the tubing is hollow it floats almost as well as a dubbed body.

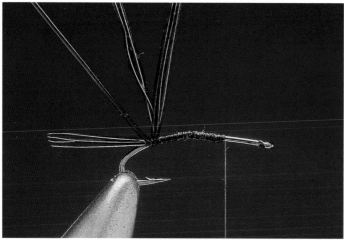

Step 1: Tie in three or four pheasant tail fibers for the tail along with the tubing for the ribbing.

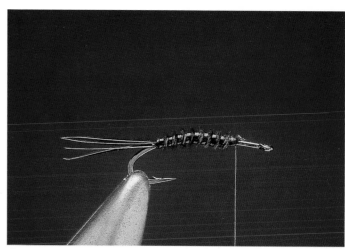

Step 2: Wrap the pheasant tail forward and then rib the body with the tubing. Make sure to leave room between each wrap of the tubing to allow some of the pheasant tail fibers to stick through. The body should end about half way up the hook shank.

Step 3: Tie in a few fibers of marabou by their tips. Twist into a rope and wrap a few times at the back of the thorax.

Step 4: Tie in a piece of the sheeting for the wing case so that it's right up against the gills.

Step 5: Tie in peacock herl by the tips and then wrap it around your thread. Wrap it forward leaving enough room for the legs and wing case.

Step 6: Cut a "V" in the partridge and tie it in so that the tips extend back just beyond the wing case.

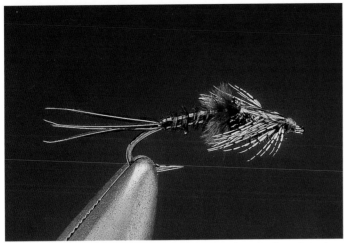 

Step 7: Pull the wing case forward, separating the legs into two equal groups and tie it down and off.

Finished Gilled Pheasant Tail (top view).

Gilled Pheasant Tail, Orange

Hook:	Targus 200, or equivalent, size 14-20
Thread:	Orange
Tail:	Orange pheasant tail
Ribbing:	Orange micro tubing or small D-Rib
Shellback:	Brown or rust
Thorax:	Peacock
Legs:	Orange pheasant tail or partridge
Gills:	Brown marabou

Gilled Pheasant Tail, Olive

Hook:	Targus 200, or equivalent, size 14-20
Thread:	Olive
Tail:	Olive pheasant tail
Ribbing:	Olive micro tubing or small D-Rib
Gills:	Olive marabou
Shellback:	Olive Flashback
Thorax:	Peacock
Legs:	Olive pheasant tail or partridge

Gilled Pheasant Tail, Black

Hook:	Targus 200, or equivalent, size 14-20
Thread:	Black
Tail:	Black pheasant tail
Ribbing:	Black micro tubing or small D-Rib
Gills:	Black marabou
Shellback:	Black or peacock Flashback
Thorax:	Peacock
Legs:	Black pheasant tail or partridge

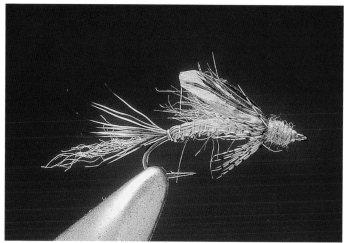

Swimming May

Hook:	Targus 200, or equivalent, size 8-16
Thread:	Match body color
Tail:	Z-lon and deer hair
Body:	Turkey biot
Ribbing:	ultra wire
Back Strap:	Deer hair
Wing:	Medallion sheeting
Thorax:	Micro dry-fly dubbing or optional bead
Legs:	Partridge

After the nymph has reached maturity, a message surges through its little body telling it that it's time to move on. The insect rests on the water's surface, where it will transform into an adult and fly away. Before this can happen though, the insect must go through another stage. Somewhere between the bottom of the stream and the surface, the nymph will start to disrobe; we will call this stage the emerger.

Most people think that this stage happens at the surface but actually it can take place anywhere between the bottom and the top of the river. This is where a wet fly or soft hackle comes in handy. Even if the insect starts to emerge at the surface, the insect can take a ride down some rapids. then it gets submerged and goes head over heels down the river. Thus, the need for wet flies.

When you see flashes of the fish feeding subsurface, it is time to try a wet fly. Try casting slightly upstream and letting the fly swim down and across from you. Generally, these strikes are not gentle and can send a shock wave right up your arm. The fish just cannot stand seeing a partially emerged insect getting away from them. A partially emerged insect is exactly what the

Swimming May fly is meant to represent. Since the wings are not at full length yet, they should be kept short in relation to the overall body. To make things a little bit more buggy looking, pull deer hair over the back and then rib it with some wire. By ribbing the deer hair with the wire the segmentations are more pronounced, as the wire compresses the hair. In addition, when the hair is pulled along the sides of the body, it gives the fly a more proportional look.

Anglers who fish wet flies today are few and far between. As mentioned earlier, by making an offering the fish have not viewed before can make a lot of difference in your success. On a spring trip to the Green River some time ago, a situation just like this occurred. The general scud and midge patterns were not working all that well and the Blue-Winged Olives were just too sparse to entice any of the fish. In the corner of one of my boxes were a couple of these wet flies, and they seemed to have some fish appeal. From this experience, that corner remains the same. It just goes to show that something new can be learned almost every time you head to the water.

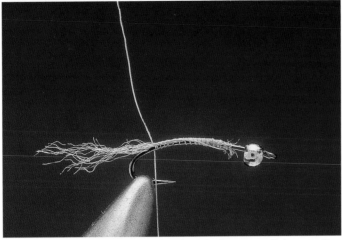

Step 1: Put a bead on the hook. Tie in some Z-lon or Ice Dubbing for the trailing shuck along with a piece of fine wire for the ribbing.

Step 2: At the bend of the hook, tie in some deer hair for the back strap.

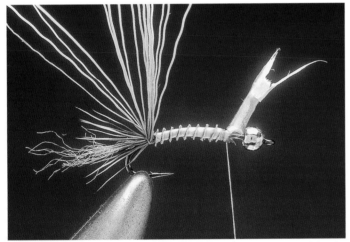

Step 3: Pull the deer hair back and then tie in a turkey biot in front of it. Place some dubbing on the hook to form an under-body and then wrap the biot over it.

Step 4: Pull the deer hair over the top and tie it down. Follow with the wire ribbing.

Step 5: Tie in some Ice Dubbing for an underwing where the body ends and then take off the thread. Push the bead back onto the underwing and reattach the thread in front of the bead. Then tie in the wing right behind the hook eye.

Step 6: Pull the wings back and to the sides of the bead and tie down. Tie in partridge or some sort of soft hackle for the legs.

Step 7: Dub the head area with some micro dry-fly dubbing or use the Ice Dubbing from the underwing. Tie off and trim the wings.

Swimming May, Brown

Hook:	Targus 200, or equivalent, size 8-16
Thread:	Brown
Tail:	Tan Z-lon and brown deer hair
Back Strap:	Brown deer hair
Ribbing:	Fine wire or brown ultra wire
Body:	Brown turkey biot
Wing:	Brown or mottled brown Medallion sheeting
Thorax:	Copper bead
Head:	Brown micro dry-fly dubbing
Legs:	Partridge

Swimming May, Olive

Hook:	Targus 200, or equivalent, size 8-16
Thread:	Olive
Tail:	Olive Z-lon and olive deer hair
Ribbing:	Fine wire or olive ultra wire
Back Strap:	Olive deer hair
Body:	Olive turkey biot
Wing:	Medium dun Medallion sheeting
Thorax:	Gold bead
Head:	Olive micro dry-fly dubbing
Legs:	Partridge

Swimming May, Gray

Hook:	Targus 200, or equivalent, size 8-16
Thread:	Gray
Tail:	Gray Z-lon and gray deer hair
Ribbing:	Fine wire or gray ultra wire
Back Strap:	Gray deer hair
Body:	Gray turkey biot
Wing:	Medium dun Medallion sheeting
Thorax:	Silver bead
Head:	Gray micro dry-fly dubbing
Legs:	Partridge

TOSHI KARITA

Medallion Biot Wet Fly

Hook:	Targus 200 or 2312, or equivalent, size 8-16
Thread:	Match the color of the body
Tail:	Partridge
Body:	Turkey biot
Underbody:	Micro dry-fly dubbing
Wing:	Medallion sheeting
Thorax:	Squirrel or hare's ear dubbing
Legs:	Partridge

Keeping on topic of the wet fly, following is a slightly different approach. The Swimming May is generally made for somewhat larger flies, like the Drakes and the *Callibaetis*. If the mayfly is placed in floatant, it can be fished in the surface film as an emerger. The Medallion Biot Wet on the other hand can be tied for the smaller to mid-sized flies. When fished in rough waters, it is a good representation of a drowned adult.

Different materials change the size of the fly. Deer hair takes up a lot of room on the shank of a hook, however by using a biot, a smaller body can be produced while still maintaining good segmentation. Although this fly's name implies that a biot is used for the body, its design is meant to allow for experimentation with new materials.

Wet flies of the past were made with floss, natural furs and quills from goose or duck. Try using a biot, midge tubing, D-Rib, or even pheasant tail fibers for the body and Medallion sheeting for the wings. Place the wings directly on top of the body and splay out the sides around the thorax. The idea is to give you a structure on which you can build. (That is, the hook and fly are tied in certain proportions.) These materials are not etched in stone with all the new materials now available experiment with some of them on some old patterns and see what happens on your next trip.

Step 1: Tie in some partridge fibers for the tail. Tie in the turkey biot by the tip with the notch facing forward. Dub a tapered underbody.

Step 2: Wrap the biot over the dubbing to about a 1/3 back from the hook eye. Add some squirrel for the thorax but leave enough room for the tie in of the wings and legs.

Step 3: Behind the hook tie in the wings spent-style, then pull them back and tie them down. Tie in some partridge for the legs on the underside of the fly.

Step 4: Dub the head and tie off. Trim the wings to shape.

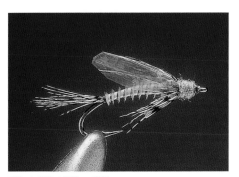

Biot Wet Fly, Olive

Hook:	Targus 200, or 2312, size 8-16
Thread:	Olive
Tail:	Partridge
Body:	Olive turkey biot
Underbody:	Olive micro dry-fly dubbing
Wing:	Medium dun Medallion sheeting
Thorax and Head:	Olive micro dry-fly dubbing
Legs:	Partridge

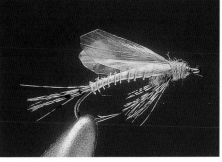

Biot Wet Fly, Tan

Hook:	Targus 200, or 2312, size 8-16
Thread:	Tan
Tail:	Partridge
Body:	*Callibaetis* turkey biot
Underbody:	*Callibaetis* micro dry-fly dubbing
Wing:	Tan Medallion sheeting
Thorax and Head:	*Callibaetis* micro dry-fly dubbing
Legs:	Partridge

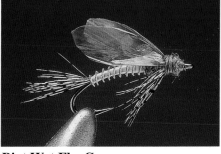

Biot Wet Fly, Gray

Hook:	Targus 200, or 2312, size 8-16
Thread:	Gray
Tail:	Partridge
Body:	Gray turkey biot
Underbody:	Gray micro dry-fly dubbing
Wing:	Medium dun or mottled gray Medallion sheeting
Thorax and Head:	Gray micro dry-fly dubbing
Legs:	Partridge

Chapter 3

EMERGERS

TOSHI KARITA

Loop Wing Emerger

Hook:	Targus 2487 or equivalent, size 14-22
Thread:	Match the body color
Tail:	Soft hackle
Body:	Hareline's Premo goose biots
Wing:	CDC
Thorax:	Micro dry-fly dubbing
Legs:	Partridge

When I first got my hands on some CDC about 10 years ago, I didn't know what to do with it. I am sure many of you have gone through this as well. One of the first things I used it for was a wing case. After all, it was being touted as a great new feather with excellent floating qualities so why not try it on a floating nymph? After I tied the first one, I noticed that the wing case was not tied down very good. When I yanked it from the vise and tossed it on the table, I noticed how different it looked standing on its head.

This first fly gave me the idea of trying to form a loop wing on purpose this time. I had never seen a fly tied like this before. If you were to view an emerger from the underside you would see that as the wing of the emerger starts to pull free from its exoskeleton, the wing tips stay tucked within the encasement as the rest of the wing pulls free. When viewed from the underside, it looks like the wings are folded over. By forming a loop wing, you achieve this enveloping process.

Not only does CDC have great floating qualities—because of its air-trapping qualities—it also adds volume to this air entrapment with the loop of the material. In my classes, I have observed how tiers struggle with forming this loop. They try to

bend the feather into shape to keep the fibers from going every which way. Don't do this, you do not want to push the feather into shape. After the tips of the CDC are tied in, stroke the fibers and stem forward over the hook eye. While the feather is pulled tight, *push* it backwards. As you do this, you can see the fibers start to spread outwards, creating the wing. It doesn't really create a loop but that's what I call it.

The Loop Wing Emerger is generally used for small to medium-sized mayflies, like the *Callibaetis* and Blue-Winged Olives, but it works great for midges. Another nice feature of this fly is that it works really well as a nymph. Just because it's called an emerger, it need not be fished only in this manner. Add some weight to your leader and fish it just like any other nymph. This is especially effective when the fly is tied in black for midges. If you're using it as an emerger in the surface film, don't put floatant on the body or the tail because the fly will float on its side and not present itself as you intended. You want the fly's body to hang down below the wing. Using a curved hook helps create this affect. Besides using biot for the body, it's also worthwhile making them with micro tubing.

Step 1: Tie in a few fibers of partridge for the tail. Leave the excess tail in place until you wrap the biot over it.

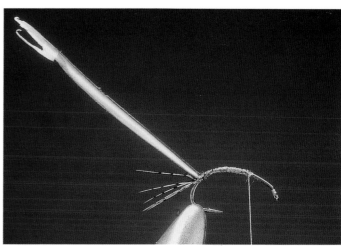

Step 2: Tie in a biot by the tip so that the notch is facing backwards.

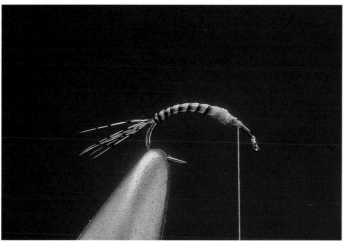

Step 3: Wrap the biot forward.

Step 4: Take two CDC feathers and even-up the tips. With the concave of the feather facing up take one fairly loose wrap around the feathers. With the thread in your right hand pull the feathers with your left hand until the tips are close to the thread. Then tighten up the thread. Tie in the CDC by the tips.

Step 5: Add dubbing to the thorax but make sure that you leave enough room for the legs and the wing to be tied in.

Step 6: Tie in the partridge for the legs so that they are on the underside of the fly.

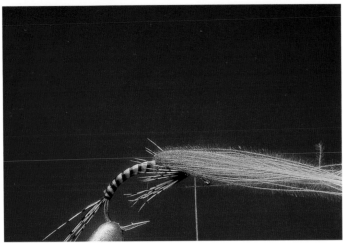

Step 7: Pull the CDC over the top so that it's tight over the thorax.

Step 8: Now, push the feathers backwards and watch the feathers spread outwards. Tie them down.

Step 9: Tie down the feathers.

Finished Loop Wing Emerger.

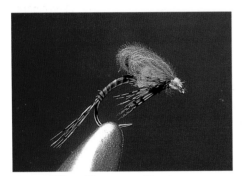

Loop Wing Emerger, Rust

Hook:	Targus 2487 or equivalent, size 14-22
Thread:	Olive
Tail:	Partridge
Body:	Hareline's Premo goose biot, red quill
Wing:	CDC
Thorax:	Yellow micro dry-fly dubbing
Legs:	Partridge

Loop Wing Emerger, Tan

Hook:	Targus 2487 or equivalent, size 14-22.
Thread:	Tan
Tail:	Partridge
Body:	Hareline's Premo goose biot, tan/dun
Wing:	CDC
Thorax:	*Callibaetis* micro dry-fly dubbing
Legs:	Partridge

Loop Wing Emerger, Brown

Hook:	Targus 2487 or equivalent, size 14-22
Thread:	Brown
Tail:	Partridge
Body:	Brown goose biot
Wing:	CDC
Thorax:	Brown micro dry-fly dubbing
Legs:	Partridge

TOSHI KARITA

Emerging Dun

Hook:	Targus 101 or equivalent, size 14-22
Thread:	Match the body color
Body:	Hareline's Premo goose biots
Shuck and Legs:	Z-lon
Wing:	Medallion sheeting or hen neck
Thorax:	Micro dry-fly dubbing

As an emerging dun floats along, its thorax splits and the new adult can be set free. The first part of the insect that comes free are the legs then the head, followed by the wings. The skin of the nymph trails behind, this is better known as the trailing shuck. When the insect is in this phase of emergence, it looks like a nymph and an adult. While this stage is occurring, the emerging dun is partially in the surface film and riding the waves fairly flat to the surface.

The tier must know these characteristics when choosing the materials for this fly. If standard dry-fly hackle were used, the fly would sit high on the surface, which is unlike the natural. However, if soft hackle or Z-lon is used for the legs, the fly would ride flush and look more natural. The wings should also mirror the natural's. They should be shorter than an adult wing but still have their shape. This is why I prefer Medallion sheeting for the wings. Plus, when the light hits the wings just right, the fly becomes visible to the angler and it's a lot easier to detect strikes.

If you're not satisfied with how something works, experiment with soft hackles. The feathers can be used for wings as well as legs. I don't know if the Emerging Dun is more effective with the soft hackle but I have a lot of confidence in that version so I probably fish it with more enthusiasm, especially if it's tied to represent Blue-Winged Olives, Pale Morning Duns and Sulphurs. We all have our favorite flies. When we try something new and it doesn't work, we tend to blame it on the fly and not ourselves. It is amazing how much more successful you are when your fly is fished with confidence.

Unlike the Loop Wing Emerger, this fly is most effective when you apply floatant since it calls for a straight-shank hook. As you can tell by the absence of hackle, this fly is best suited to spring-creek type waters, otherwise you probably wouldn't have a clue where the fly is. Then again, if you wish to try it in less-than-ideal conditions, by all means, use some hackle. When using hackle, I like to wrap it through the thorax before the wings are mounted and then pull the hackle fibers from the bottom to the sides, or even cut a "V" in the bottom. By doing this, the fly once again be used on those tranquil waters. In other words, if hackle is used, the fly is more versatile than if it were left out.

Step 1: Take the thread up to the hook eye and tie in several fibers of Z-lon so that it extends out over the eye. Wrap the thread backwards over the excess until you get to the bend of the hook for the shuck. The legs and shuck are one piece.

Step 2: Tie in a biot by the tip and with the notch facing backwards. Then wrap it forward. The body should be about 1/4 back from the hook eye.

Step 3: Cut a strip of the sheeting to the width you would like your wings to be. Tie them in slightly behind the legs. Remember, emerger wings are narrower and shorter than adult wings.

Step 4: Dub in back of and around the wings to form the thorax.

Step 5: As you start to dub in front of the wings, pull the wings back and tie them down with a couple of turns of the dubbing.

Step 6: Before the head area gets too big, divide the legs into two equal groups and tie them down along the sides of the thorax. Cut them to the length of the hook point.

Finished Emerging Dun.

A variation using a different shuck, wing, and some hackle.

Emerging Dun, Tan

Hook:	Targus 101 or equivalent, size 14-22
Thread:	Tan
Shuck:	Tan Z-lon
Body:	Hareline's Premo goose biot tan/dun
Wing:	Tan Medallion sheeting
Thorax:	*Callibaetis* micro dry-fly dubbing
Legs:	Tan Z-lon

Emerging Dun, Brown

Hook:	Targus 101 or equivalent, size 14-22
Thread:	Brown
Shuck:	Tan Z-lon
Body:	Brown goose biot
Wing:	Tan Medallion sheeting
Thorax:	Brown micro dry-fly dubbing
Legs:	Tan Z-lon

Emerging Dun, Sulphur Yellow

Hook:	Targus 101 or equivalent, size 14-22
Thread:	Yellow
Shuck:	Yellow Z-lon
Body:	Hareline's Premo goose biot, Sulphur yellow
Wing:	Dun/yellow Medallion sheeting
Thorax:	Yellow micro dry-fly dubbing
Legs:	Yellow Z-lon

TOSHI KARITA

Green Drake Emerger

Hook:	Targus 2312 or equivalent size 10-14
Thread:	Match the color of the body
Shuck:	Z-lon
Body:	Single-strand white floss colored with a Chartpak marker, celery or pale olive
Ribbing:	Micro tubing
Underwing:	Ice Dubbing
Wing:	Medallion sheeting
Thorax:	Awesome Possum dubbing
Legs:	Partridge

Out West where the Rockies reach to the heavens, a midsummer mayfly hatch occurs warranting just as much admiration. The Green Drake is a big fly by all standards. Colorado is not the only place these insects are found, you will find them on the Henry's Fork in Idaho as well as the Metolius River in Oregon, where my videos were filmed.

The Green Drakes in the Frying Pan River are different from the others. When it first hatches, the process takes place at the bottom of the stream, out of sight of the angler. This doesn't happen in every instance but nevertheless this possibility should be kept in mind. Once again, knowing something about the actual insect can increase your success and put you that much more ahead of the game. When the Drake hatches, it pulls free from its shuck and swims to the surface. Fish key in on this journey and ignore all else. The large wings are laid back over its pale body giving off a silvery, glistening effect. This look can be achieved with Medallion sheeting and Ice Dubbing for the wing. This is probably the most eye-catching—and therefore fish-attracting—feature of the fly. Using synthetic materials provides a more translucent effect. Natural materials fall short.

Any newly hatched insect is pale and drab in comparison to its adult colors. When choosing a material for the body, keep this in mind. Keep in mind too, the material will darken when it gets wet. If you use white floss, any color can be applied with a Chartpak marker.

The ribbing, which is very pronounced on the Green Drake, requires special attention too. Generally, the segmentations or ribbings are a brownish color, the ones on the Frying Pan lean towards rust. Placing rust-colored tubing over the floss body gives a very realistic appearance. This is even more evident when the body becomes wet.

Fish the Green Drake Emerger in the same manner you would fish any emerger, placing floatant on it and fishing it in the film. However, since this fly can also emerge at the streams bottom, you can try another approach. This emerger can be fished like a traditional wet fly or even a nymph with added weight placed on the leader. When using weight, as the fly tumbles along the bottom of the river, swim the fly to the surface in the same manner you would a caddis pattern. With a mouthful of this fly passing by a hungry fish, the results can be amazing.

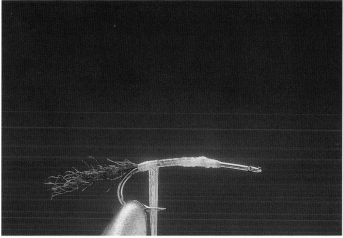

Step 1: Tie in several strands of Z-lon so that it extends out the back of the fly for the shuck.

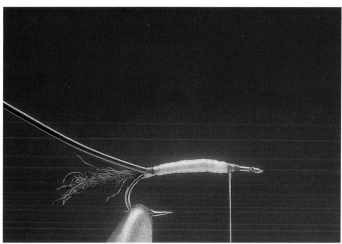

Step 2: Tie in the tubing for the ribbing and form a tapered body with the floss. The body should end about a 1/4 of the way back from the hook eye.

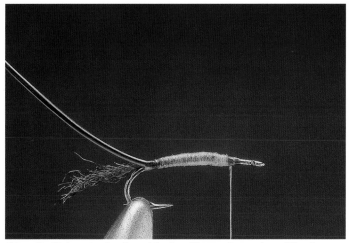

Step 3: Color the body with the Chartpak marker. The longer you go over the body with the marker, the darker it will get.

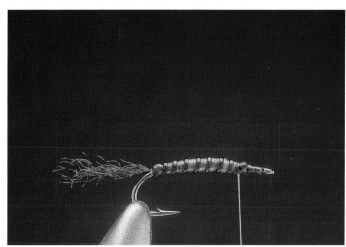

Step 4: Rib the body with the tubing. The greater you stretch the tubing, the more translucent it will become.

Step 5: Tie in some Ice Dubbing for the underwing.

Step 6: Cut a strip of the sheeting to the width you want your wings to be, then tie them in behind the hook eye.

Step 7: Pull the wings back along the sides of the thorax and tie them down. Tie in some partridge for the legs so that they are on the underside of the fly.

Step 8: Dub the head.

Step 9: Trim the wings to shape. The Drake's wing length is longer than usual so make them the length of the body or just a little longer.

TOSHI KARITA

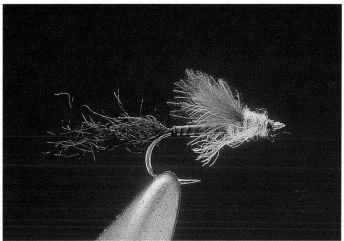

CDC Emerging Dun

Hook:	Targus 101 or equivalent, size 14-20
Thread:	Match the body color
Shuck:	Z-lon or Ice Dubbing
Body:	Hareline's Premo goose biots
Wing:	CDC
Thorax:	Micro dry-fly dubbing
Legs:	Z-lon

When it come to emergers, the CDC feather has become the first choice for fly tiers. It's the perfect color (dun) and is easy to use. You can also use just the tips of the feathers, giving a more clean look, or you can simply pull the fibers from the stem and tie them in. Once the clump of CDC is tied in, it can be trimmed to any shape and size that you wish. The best part is that even when you do trim it, the feather still looks natural and, more importantly, it still works.

This particular fly represents an emerger resting in or on the surface as it finishes its emergence. This is the reason for using a straight-shank hook. For this phase, the fly should lay flat on the surface and not stand above it. Thus, the absence of hackle. Instead, use Z-lon for the legs. Another option is to use soft hackle for the legs. Recently, I have been using more and more of this feather because of its softness and movement in the water. In addition, the available colors one has to choose from are always interesting.

The CDC Emerging Dun is pretty much like the previous Emerging Dun except that this uses CDC. The CDC gives a good wing silhouette and holds the fly in the top part of the surface film. Also, with its air-trapping qualities, tiny air bubbles can form and adhere to the feather, yet another feature which lets this fly stand out from the rest. To make the wings a little more pronounced, after the feathers have been tied in take a few turns of thread around the base of each feather. This will separate them into two individual wings and also help stabilize the fly on the surface. Once this is done, the wings can be trimmed down to the length and shape of a mayfly wing. Just remember that you are not creating an adult pattern with full-blown wings. The wings should be shorter than the body, making them look as if they are just emerging from the shuck.

To fish this fly, do not use any liquid paste on it. Liquids and paste will destroy the air-trapping qualities of the CDC rendering it useless. To this day, I still like to use Top Ride or Blue Ribbon on my CDC flies. They are both a desiccant in the form of a powder so no damage to the feather will result. As a side note, a fellow CDC enthusiast, Ben Nelson, has suggested that Aquel be used, even though it is a liquid. He suggests that a little bit of this stuff can be put onto your fingers and worked into the CDC. Then you kind of dab it dry with a paper towel. I have yet to try it but I take Ben at his word. All three of these products are made by Loon Outdoors and should be available at your local fly shop.

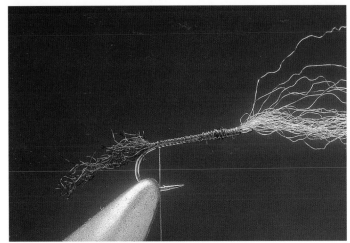

Step 1: Right behind the eye of the hook, tie in some Z-lon so that it sticks out over the eye of the hook. Tie in a different colored Z-lon for the shuck if you wish, and have it extend out the back. Trim the shuck.

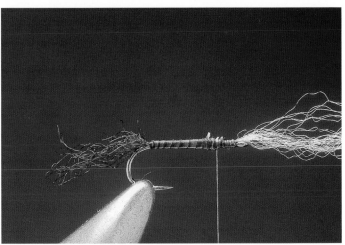

Step 2: Tie in a biot by the tip and so that the notch is facing backward and then wrap the biot forward. You should be about 1/3 the way back from the hook eye.

Step 3: Form the back portion of the thorax out of the dubbing. Then take two CDC feathers and even-up the tips. Tie them in so that the tips reach the end of the body.

Step 4: Front view showing the wings split.

Step 5: Trim the wing to shape and then place some dubbing in front of and onto the wing. Before you finish off the head area though, split the legs into two equal group and pull them along the side of the fly. Now you can finish off the head area with some more dubbing.

Finished CDC Emerging Dun.

The same fly with hackle instead of Z-lon for the legs. The hackle is tied in after the biot is wrapped and brought forward before the wing is put into place.

CDC Emerging Dun, Gray

Hook:	Targus 101 or equivalent, size 14-20
Thread:	Gray
Tail:	Gray Z-lon
Body:	Hareline's Premo goose biot, gray dun
Wing:	CDC
Thorax and Head:	Gray micro dry-fly dubbing
Legs:	Gray Z-lon

CDC Emerging Dun, Tan

Hook:	Targus 101 or equivalent, size 14-20
Thread:	Tan
Tail:	Tan Z-lon
Body:	Hareline's Premo goose biot, tan dun
Wing:	CDC
Thorax and Head:	*Callibaetis* micro dry-fly dubbing
Legs:	Tan Z-lon

CDC Emerging Dun, Olive

Hook:	Targus 101 or equivalent, size 14-20
Thread:	Olive
Tail:	Gray Z-lon
Body:	Hareline's Premo goose biot Blue-Winged Olive
Wing:	CDC
Thorax and Head:	Blue-Winged Olive micro dry-fly dubbing
Legs:	Gray Z-lon

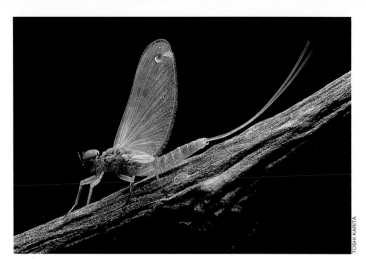

CDC Emerger

Hook:	Targus 2487 or equivalent, size 12-20
Thread:	Match the body color
Body:	Hareline's Premo goose biots
Wing:	CDC
Thorax:	Micro dry-fly dubbing
Legs:	Partridge

This emerger is tied on a curved-shank hook so that the fly's body hangs down below the wing in the surface film. It's a good little fly to show yet another way in which CDC can be used for an emerger wing.

Basically, there are two different shapes for emergers. The straight-bodied one that was just shown in the Emerging Dun and the curve-bodied fly that is being shown here. As the nymph starts to pull free from its shuck, it does so on the surface or within the surface film. The tension at the surface can be great enough that the tiny nymph won't break through completely and will rest for a period. That is when the curved-shank hook style works the best.

To keep the fly's body hanging below the wings, carefully apply the floatant. If floatant is placed on a body that is curved, the body will float on its side and not give a good presentation. So, take one more step when dressing this fly by placing saliva on your fingertips and rubbing it over the body and tail or shuck. This will

remove any floatant that may have found its way there and give the fly a chance to work in the manner in which it was designed.

It's important to keep the shuck or tailing material fairly sparse on these flies so that it does not ride on the surface and fall on its side. Notice that the wings are tied a little differently on this fly compared to the Emerging Dun. Previously, the wings were tied in and separated so that they were each held apart. On the CDC Emerger, the wings are tied in so that they marry together and form one wing. The wings still have an emergent appearance but can also be viewed as a cripple, so if it rides on its side, it's OK. After all, many naturals find themselves trying to free a wing that has become trapped in the surface film. This fly's balance is not as great as its sister is, the Emerging Dun. The fly has a tendency to teeter back and forth as it floats down the river, the wing holds it in the surface film.

Step 1: Tie in some partridge fibers for the tail, then tie in the biot by the tip with the notch facing backward. Wrap the biot forward.

Step 2: Place a small amount of dubbing at the back of the thorax. Take two CDC feathers, even up the tips and tie them in. They should extend back past the tail.

Step 3: Trim the wing to shape and tie in some partridge for the legs on the underside of the fly.

Step 4: Dub the head area and tie off.

CDC Emerger, Olive

Hook:	Targus 2487 or equivalent, size 12-20
Thread:	Olive
Tail:	Partridge
Body:	Hareline's Premo goose biot, olive dun
Wing:	CDC
Thorax:	Blue-winged Olive micro dry-fly dubbing
Legs:	Partridge

CDC Emerger, Tan

Hook:	Targus 2487 or equivalent, size 12-20
Thread:	Tan
Tail:	Partridge
Body:	Hareline's Premo goose biot, tan dun
Wing:	CDC
Thorax:	*Callibaetis* micro dry-fly dubbing
Legs:	Partridge

CDC Emerger, Rust

Hook:	Targus 2487 or equivalent, size 12-20
Thread:	Olive
Tail:	Partridge
Body:	Hareline's Premo goose biot red quill
Wing:	CDC
Thorax:	Yellow micro dry-fly dubbing
Legs:	Partridge

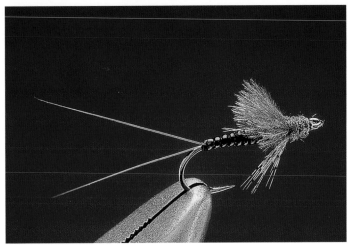

JIM SCHOLLMEYER

RS-2 Emerger

Hook:	Targus 101 or 200, size 14-22
Thread:	Match the color of the body
Tail:	Mayfly tails
Body:	Small D-Rib
Wing:	CDC
Thorax:	Micro dry-fly dubbing
Legs:	Partridge

This is one of those flies that has been around forever. Rim Chung first introduced this little gem almost 30 years ago. Rim's Semblance #2 was the result of the continued pursuit of a simple mayfly/nymph/emerger pattern that could be used during any hatch. Mr. Chung's contribution to fly fishing is greatly appreciated. Because of his efforts, we all can fish a simple fly that works.

The key to this fly lies in its ability to mimic most insects found in our rivers. This includes Blue-Winged Olives, Pale Morning Duns, Tricos, and Sulphurs. The RS-2 Emerger can be considered a nymph or an emerger. Here, it will be referred to as an emerger. The wing utilizes CDC in two ways: First, the natural dun color is perfect; second, is its floatability. The fibers are pulled from the stem and tied in a clump in the thorax area. When the dubbing is placed around it, you can make the wing stand straight up by placing some of the dubbing in front of or behind it. You might also choose to have the wing lie flat. For this shape, wrap the dubbing onto the front of the wing.

While the CDC fibers are still long and uncut, pull some of the fibers down along the sides of the thorax for legs. Be careful not to tie them down when you dub around the wing. This way, more of the feather can be utilized, minimizing waste. I like to use partridge for the legs. They are tapered to a fine point, have

barrings built into the fibers, and the feather is soft. When it comes to tying nymphs and emergers, I find it hard not to incorporate some partridge into my flies.

The body is another area in which this fly differs from the original. If I am planning on using it exclusively as a nymph, I tie the body with D-Rib. Since it is a solid material it tends to be a bit heavier and less prone to floating. However, if I am planning on fishing the fly as an emerger, or as an all-purpose fly, I use the micro tubing. The tubing is hollow so air will get trapped in it, helping it to float.

This is one of those flies guides love because they're so easy to tie. As previously mentioned, it can be fished as a nymph or an emerger. For a nymph, just add a little weight to your leader so the fly sinks down to the level in which the fish are feeding. For an emerger, put some floatant on it, and don't worry about getting it on your CDC wing. Also, try tying this fly on a curved hook to change things a little bit. The fly is built with such a minimal amount of materials that its weight is not a concern. Find a fish that is rising and try a cast or two into its feeding lane. If the fish is receptive to emergers, this fly will generally draw a response. For an all-around rig set up, trail this fly behind an adult pattern. If the first fly doesn't get fish, the second one will. Thank you, Mr. Chung.

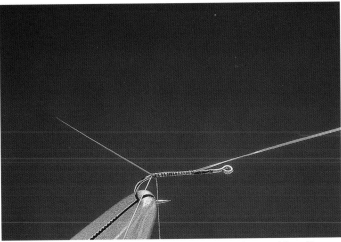

Step 1: Tie in two mayfly tails and separate them with a figure-eight.

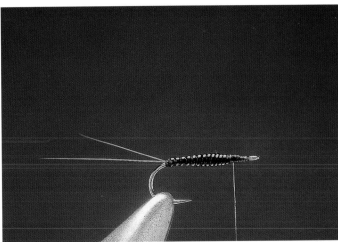

Step 2: Cut the D-Rib at an angle and tie it in. With the thread, form an underbody which tapers from the back to the front. Wrap the D-Rib forward. The body should end about 1/3 the way back from the hook eye.

Step 3: Place a small amount of dubbing at the back of the thorax. Pull some CDC from the stem and tie it in, you can use the tips if you wish. Trim to a length just above the hook barb or hook point.

Step 4: Tie in some partridge for the legs so that the fibers lay along the sides of the thorax.

Dub the head and tie off.

Finished RS-2 Emerger.

RS-2 Emerger, Gray

Hook:	Targus 101, or 200, size 14-22
Thread:	Gray
Tail:	Dark dun mayfly tails
Body:	Small gray D-Rib or micro tubing
Wing:	CDC
Thorax:	Gray micro dry-fly dubbing
Legs:	Partridge

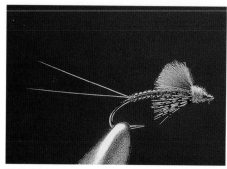

RS-2 Emerger, Tan

Hook:	Targus 101, or 200, size 14-22
Thread:	Tan
Tail:	Tan mayfly tails
Body:	Small tan D-Rib or micro tubing
Wing:	CDC
Thorax:	*Callibaetis* micro dry-fly dubbing
Legs:	Partridge

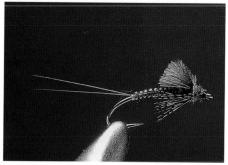

RS-2 Emerger, Olive

Hook:	Targus 101, or 200, size 14-22
Thread:	Olive
Tail:	Dark dun mayfly tails
Body:	Small olive D-Rib or micro tubing
Wing:	CDC
Thorax:	*Callibaetis* micro dry-fly dubbing
Legs:	Partridge

80

JIM SCHOLLMEYER

Winger Emerger

Hook:	Targus 2487 or equivalent, size 12-22
Thread:	Match the body color
Tail:	Soft hackle
Body:	Micro tubing
Wing:	Hen neck
Hackle:	Soft hackle
Thorax:	Micro dry-fly dubbing

Having confidence in the flies that you use does more to increase your success than anything else you do. If you do not have confidence in what you are using, you probably are not going to fish it correctly or with much enthusiasm and the results will show.

What does confidence have to do with this fly? Well, it was with this thought in mind that it was created. If you browse through my catalogs, or even this book, you will find other flies that look similar but that use synthetics. As a commercial fly tier, I get requests from around the country and I try to keep up with what anglers want in their materials and flies. For many, the use of synthetics is strictly taboo. Knowing this, I produced some flies tied with all natural materials. This is basically the only reason I developed this fly. Does it work better than the flies tied with medallion wings? I don't think so, but then again that's the fly in which I have the most confidence. Others will have greater success with this fly because their confidence level is higher.

The nice thing about the Winger is that the materials for tying it are fairly cheap. Cheap compared to using regular dry-fly hackle. Hen necks have been around forever but, for the most part, are seldom used. However, when you have a genetic wizard, like Dr.

Tom Whiting, new possibilities are achieved. Mostly, hen necks have been used for wings, which is reflected in A.K. Best's flies. This fly, however, uses it as hackle. The soft hackles that are available are longer and narrower than ever before, making them ideal for hackles. Plus, the natural and dyed colors in which these feathers come, would make Van Gogh drool with delight.

The body material can be D-Rib, micro tubing, or what is used here, goose biot. Since goose biots are not all that long, they should be used for flies size 16 and smaller. If you really want to use biots for the body, and the flies you are tying are larger than a 16, turkey can be used. Even though turkey does not have the same definite segmentations as goose, at least you are using natural materials.

As mentioned before, on curved-hooked flies, floatant should not be placed on the body. Other than that, this fly can be fished just like any other emerger. Remember, the Green Drake Emerger and the RS-2 can also be fished as a nymph or a wet fly. Do not bind yourself by always following the conventional methods of fishing emergers or dries strictly as they were intended. Get creative when fishing them. Mother Nature is not always perfect either, her creations are, at times, less than perfect.

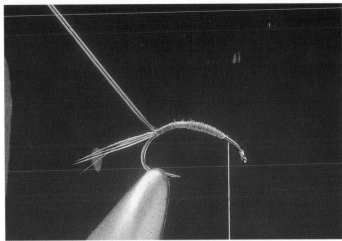

Step 1: Tie in a few fibers of soft hackle for the tail. Then cut the tubing at an angle and tie it in.

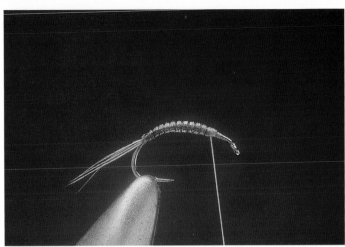

Step 2: Wrap the tubing forward so that you are about 1/3 the way back from the hook eye.

Step 3: Tie in the hackle and place some dubbing in the thorax.

Step 4: Wrap the hackle through the thorax but leave enough room at the head to tie in the wings.

Step 5: Tie in the wings so that they fan out away from each other and tie off. On larger flies, like the one shown, tie down the wings further back onto the thorax and dub a head.

Finished Winger Emerger.

Winger Emerger, Tan

Hook:	Targus 2487 or equivalent, size 12-20
Thread:	Tan
Tail:	Tan soft hackle or partridge
Body:	Small tan D-Rib or micro tubing
Wing:	Hen neck
Hackle:	Whiting's *Callibaetis* or equivalent
Thorax:	*Callibaetis* micro dry-fly dubbing

Winger Emerger, Rust

Hook:	Targus 2487 or equivalent, size 12-20
Thread:	Olive
Tail:	Tan soft hackle or partridge
Body:	Small rust D-Rib or micro tubing
Wing:	Hen neck
Hackle:	Whiting's pale morning dun or equivalent
Thorax:	Yellow micro dry-fly dubbing

Winger Emerger, Olive

Hook:	Targus 2487 or equivalent, size 12-20
Thread:	Olive
Tail:	Olive soft hackle or partridge
Body:	Small olive D-Rib or micro tubing
Wing:	Hen neck
Hackle:	Whiting's blue-winged olive or equivalent
Thorax:	Blue-winged olive micro dry-fly dubbing

Ice Emerger

Hook:	Targus 2487 or equivalent, size 14-24
Thread:	Match the body color
Tail:	Partridge
Body:	Micro tubing
Wing:	Ice Dubbing
Thorax:	Micro dry-fly dubbing

Does this fly look familiar? Of course it does. It is more or less a curved RS-2 Ice-Dubbed emerger. That's the thing with new materials, once they arrive at the fly shop, we just have to have them. Then we get home, have a beer and stare at the vise. The new purchases always find their way into some of our old patterns and that is basically what has happened here. When I first received the Ice Dub, I said, "Wow." The possibilities running through my head were endless. I knew this material would work great for an emerger wing.

The Loop Wing Emerger, which is formed out of CDC, has already been done but why not use this material in the same manner? Nothing ventured, nothing gained, as they say. Well, the Ice Dubbing works pretty well for the formation of a loop wing, but to make things easier I trim it to length. This way, a size 24 can be tied with no problem (as long as you can see it) and the effect is pretty much the same.

Because of its simplistic and sparse design, this fly is ideal for fishing small fly hatches, such as Blue-Winged Olives,

Pseudocloeons, and even midges. Although its name implies emerger, it is best fished as a nymph. By fishing it this way, larger and more fish are caught, however the thrill of seeing a nose rise to your offering is not there. Nymphing on such rivers as the South Platte and San Juan is the method of choice. If the crowds have elbowed you out of the main holes, be observant and watch the edges of the riffles for some risers. If any are spotted, drift this emerger right over their nose and see what happens. The fish may not be as large but the thrill of your fly disappearing under a swirl is well worth it.

When fishing the Ice Emerger in the surface, try it with and without floatant. Although you may not be able to see the fish take your fly, a small fly like this fished wet, submerged below the surface, may be just the offering the fish are looking for. To detect strikes, a small indicator can be used roughly three feet above the fly. Nevertheless, it is best if you hone your casting skills and figure out the general area in which you think your fly should be in for drawing rises.

Step 1: Tie in a few fibers of partridge for the tail. Then cut the tubing at an angle and tie it in.

Step 2: Wrap the tubing forward so that you are about 1/4 the way back from the hook eye.

84

Step 3: Place a little bit of the dubbing at the back of the thorax, then tie in the Ice Dubbing for the wing.

Step 4: Tie in some partridge for the legs so that the fibers are on the underside of the fly.

Step 5: Finish dubbing the head and tie off.

Ice Emerger, Olive

Hook:	Targus 2487 or equivalent, size 14-24
Thread:	Olive
Tail:	Partridge
Body:	Small olive D-Rib or micro tubing
Wing:	UV olive Ice Dubbing
Thorax:	Blue-winged olive micro dry-fly dubbing
Legs:	Partridge

Ice Emerger, Black

Hook:	Targus 2487 or equivalent, size 14-24
Thread:	Black
Body:	Small black D-Rib or micro tubing
Wing:	UV gray Ice Dubbing
Thorax:	Black micro dry-fly dubbing
Legs:	Partridge

Ice Emerger, Brown

Hook:	Targus 2487 or equivalent, size 14-24
Thread:	Brown
Tail:	Partridge
Body:	Small brown D-Rib or micro tubing
Wing:	UV tan Ice Dubbing
Thorax:	Brown micro dry-fly dubbing
Legs:	Partridge

Deer Dun Emerger

Hook:	Targus 101 or equivalent, size 10-16
Thread:	Match the body color
Body:	Hareline's Premo goose biots
Shuck:	Hareline's Trailing Shucks
Wing:	Medallion sheeting
Legs:	Deer hair
Thorax:	Micro dry-fly dubbing

Emergers and dry flies, for the most part, contain hackle for the legs and floatation. But, have you checked out the price of some of the top-quality hackles lately? Sure, saddle hackles and cut up portions of a neck make it more bearable but I think you get the point.

Deer hair helps relieve some of this financial stress. The deer hair is tied in on the underside of the fly with thread interwoven among the fibers. This placement of the thread within the deer hair spreads out the fibers, making it look and act like hackle. Remember, hackle is meant to look like the legs of an adult and give it some floatation. Whatever material is used, hackle or deer hair, the fibers spread out and redistribute the weight of the fly along its fibers. Think of how it feels when a woman in pumps steps on your hand with the heel. It smarts! However, when she steps on your hand with the front part of the shoe, you feel pressure instead of pain because the weight is distributed over a greater area.

The rest of the Deer Dun Emerger is basically the same as the Emerging Dun. However, this fly shows yet another way in which one can imitate a trailing shuck. For this fly I use one of Hareline's Trailing Shucks. These are one of the most exact imitations of a shuck ever commercially produced. Just take it from the package and tie it onto your hook. That's it. They are translucent and come complete with segmentations. The most versatile color is the clear, you can use a Chartpak marker to make them whatever color you desire. For additional insights into using these shucks, as well as others, see Tying Trailing Shucks, page 18.

Since there is no hackle on the bottom of the fly to help support it, this particular type of fly is best used in calmer waters. It is not meant for whitewater searches. Since CDC is not used on this fly, you can use your favorite floatant without worrying about matting down any fibers. The nicest feature of this fly is the deer hair. It has a good earth-tone color, it tapers from the base to the tip, just like natural legs, and it's cheap. For more instruction on tying this fly, my video, "Tying Mayflies," will help. The video has close-up shots on how to tie in the deer hair.

Step 1: Tie a Hareline Trailing Shuck onto the hook shank.

Step 2: Tie in a biot by the tip, with the notch facing backward. Then wrap the biot forward.

Step 3: Cut a strip of the sheeting to the width you'd like for your wings, then tie them in right behind the hook eye. From the wing back to where you tied off the biot, wrap some dubbing for the thorax.

Step 4: Stack some deer hair and pinch it against the side of the thorax away from you. As you take the thread over it and cinch down on it, the deer hair should roll underneath the fly where we want it. Cut off the excess deer and cover it with some dubbing.

Step 5: Pull some of the deer hair back along each side of the thorax and tie down. Move the thread forward a little bit and repeat the steps.

Step 6: Pull the wings back and tie them down. Then take your thread to the hook eye and tie off. The deer hair should be sticking out the sides of the thorax, so if any fibers are on the bottom trim them off.

Finished Deer Dun Emerger.

Top view.

Deer Dun Emerger, Brown

Hook:	Targus 101 or equivalent, size 10-16
Thread:	Brown
Shuck:	Hareline's tan Trailing Shuck
Body:	Brown goose biot
Wing:	Brown Medallion sheeting
Thorax:	Brown micro dry-fly dubbing
Legs:	Brown deer hair

Deer Dun Emerger, Olive

Hook:	Targus 101 or equivalent, size 10-16
Thread:	Olive
Shuck:	Hareline's gray Trailing Shucks
Body:	Hareline's Premo goose biot, Blue-Winged Olive
Wing:	Medium dun Medallion sheeting
Thorax:	Blue-Winged Olive micro dry-fly dubbing
Legs:	Olive deer hair

Deer Dun Emerger, Tan

Hook:	Targus 101 or equivalent, size 10-16
Thread:	Tan
Shuck:	Hareline's tan Trailing Shucks
Body:	Hareline's Premo goose biot tan/dun
Wing:	Tan Medallion sheeting
Thorax:	*Callibaetis* micro dry-fly dubbing
Legs:	Natural deer hair

TOSHI KARITA

Parachute Emerging Dun

Hook:	Targus 2487 or equivalent, size 12-20
Thread:	Match body color
Shuck:	Z-lon or Ice Dubbing
Body:	Hairline's Premo goose biots
Wing:	CDC
Hackle:	Dry fly
Thorax:	Micro dry-fly dubbing

When it comes to adult mayfly patterns, parachutes far out-sell and are more widely used than most conventionally hackled dry flies. So why not use this same tying technique for emergers? When parachuting emergers, a lot of hackle is not needed. Just a few wraps of hackle will more than suffice for flotation. Remember, you want the fly to ride fairly flush in the surface film.

Instead of using a straight-shank hook for a parachute emerger, a curved shank seems to work better. A trailing shuck made of the most appropriate materials can be added so that it will sink below the thorax. Most parachute patterns have you wrapping the hackle around a post which is supposed to imitate a wing, but I think it is best served as an indicator. For something different, try wrapping the hackle around your shellback material, which in this case is CDC, and leave the excess wing case for a wing. By wrapping your hackle in this manner and then pulling the wing case forward, the hackle is scarce in the front of the fly. This gives the appearance that the hackle is coming out of the sides of the thorax, like legs, when viewed from the underside. The body material really doesn't matter but I like to use micro tubing, like in the sample shown, or goose biots. The tubing can be used on larger flies plus it has the translucence that I like for many of my flies.

Since CDC is used for the wing and wing case, liquid floatants should be avoided. If you want, you can use some Z-lon or poly yarn in place of the CDC and then any type of floatant can be used.

Step 1: Tie in some Z-lon starting at the back of the thorax and tying down on to the bend of the hook. Cut it short and round it off if you wish.

Step 2: Tie in a biot by the tip and with the notch facing backward. Wrap the biot forward.

Step 3: Take two or three CDC feathers and even up the tips. Tie them in so that the tips extend back about twice the length of the body. Tie in the hackle.

Step 4: Wrap the hackle around the base of the CDC feathers and tie off. Pull the wing back and dub the thorax.

Step 5: With your right hand, grab the CDC and with your left grab and pull back the hackle. As you pull back the hackle, pull forward on the CDC and tie down right behind the hook eye. With the CDC out over the hook eye, pull it back and tie down again.

View from the underside.

Parachute Emerging Dun, Gray

Hook:	Targus 2487 or equivalent, size 12-20
Thread:	Gray
Tail:	Gray soft hackle or partridge
Body:	Hareline's Premo goose biot gray dun
Wing:	CDC
Hackle:	Medium dun
Thorax:	Gray micro dry-fly dubbing

Parachute Emerging Dun, Tan

Hook:	Targus 2487 or equivalent, size 12-20
Thread:	Tan
Tail:	Tan soft hackle or partridge
Body:	Hareline's Premo goose biot tan/dun
Wing:	CDC
Hackle:	Whiting's *Callibaetis* or equivalent
Thorax:	*Callibaetis* micro dry-fly dubbing

Parachute Emerging Dun, Olive

Hook:	Targus 2487 or equivalent, size 12-20
hread:	Olive
Tail:	Olive soft hackle or partridge
Body:	Hareline's Premo goose biot, olive dun
Wing:	CDC
Hackle:	Whiting's blue-winged olive or equivalent
Thorax:	Blue-winged olive micro dry-fly dubbing

TOSHI KARITA

CDC Floating Emerger

Hook:	Targus 101 or equivalent, size 12-20
Thread:	Match body color
Tail:	Crimped mayfly tails
Body:	Micro tubing
Ribbing:	FisHair
Thorax:	Micro dry-fly dubbing
Hackle:	Hen neck
Wing:	CDC

Most "new" flies are really just variations on flies that have been used for years. This fly is no different. At first glance this fly resembles the Hair Wing Dun that fly tier extraordinaire, René Harrop, created years ago. The Hair Wing Dun has enjoyed many years of success, so why mess with it? With the abundance of new materials, why not try them in place of some of the older materials? For me, experimenting with new materials is part of the fun in fly tying.

The tail has been crimped with hemostats to make the tail look somewhat crippled and the body is made out of micro tubing. For those who like to use natural materials, goose biots work pretty well also. Since this fly is tied on a straight-shank hook, the fly can actually represent a dun pattern as well as an emerger.

This gives the angler more options in their presentation of the fly.

The wing can be tied in by using just the tips of the CDC or by pulling the fibers off the stem and then tying them in. Once the wing is tied in, I like to round them off a little bit so that the wing is actually shaped like a natural's wing. In recent years, I have become increasingly more attracted to soft hackles for my emergers rather than standard hackles. The soft hackle only requires a wrap or two and, more importantly, it has some movement on the water. The body can be made from micro tubing, like this example, or it can be formed from goose biot. If I do use the biot, however, I like the body to be smooth and not have the fuzzy rib from the leading edge of the biot. It doesn't make any difference to the fish but I think it looks more natural.

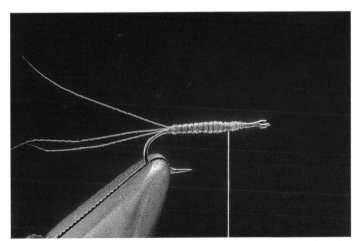

Step 1: Crimp three mayfly tails in a pair of hemostats. Cut the tubing at an angle and tie it in as well as the ribbing. Wrap the tubing forward and then the ribbing. You should be about 1/3 the way back from the hook eye.

Step 2: Tie in the hackle and then dub the thorax. Wrap the hackle forward through the thorax and cut the hackle flat on top of the fly.

Step 3: Take two to three CDC feathers and even up the tips. Tie them down behind the hook eye so that the tips are sticking back to the end of the body.

Step 4: Cut the excess off flush with the hook eye and trim the wing to shape.

Top view.

CDC Floating Emerger, Yellow

Hook:	Targus 101 or equivalent, size 12-20
Thread:	Yellow
Tail:	Yellow mayfly tails crimped
Body:	Yellow micro tubing
Wing:	CDC
Hackle:	Whiting's Pale Morning Dun or equivalent
Thorax:	Yellow micro dry-fly dubbing

CDC Floating Emerger, Gray

Hook:	Targus 101 or equivalent, size 12-20
Thread:	Gray
Tail:	Dark dun mayfly tails crimped
Body:	Gray micro tubing
Wing:	CDC
Hackle:	Medium dun
Thorax:	Gray micro dry-fly dubbing

CDC Floating Emerger, Olive

Hook:	Targus 101 or equivalent, size 12-20
Thread:	Olive
Tail:	Dark dun mayfly tails crimped
Body:	Olive micro tubing
Wing:	CDC
Hackle:	Whiting's Blue-Winged Olive or equivalent
Thorax:	Blue-Winged Olive micro dry-fly dubbing

TOSHI KARITA

Twisted Hackle Emerger

Hook:	Targus 2487 or equivalent, size 12-22
Thread:	Color to match body
Shuck:	Z-lon
Body:	Hareline's Premo goose biots
Hackle:	When possible use a saddle hackle
Thorax:	Micro dry-fly dubbing
Wing:	Natural CDC

If you were to straighten out the hook on this fly, it looks a lot like the Floating Emerger. However, there are a few alterations and a somewhat different approach to hackling involved in this fly.

To start with, the tail has been replaced with Z-lon for a trailing shuck. The body can be whatever you wish, dubbing, biot or micro tubing. To add some life to the fly, marabou is tied in and wrapped for gills before the thorax is formed. Then we come to the hackle.

The hackle on most emergers is either wrapped through the thorax or some type of parachute is used. The hackles on this fly however is wrapped around some dubbed thread and then it's wrapped forward. Why do this? Just as peacock is wrapped around the thread for strength, the hackle can be too. One note,

saddle hackle works best because the hackle's stem is more slender than regular hackle and is less likely to break. Adding dubbing on the thread before this is done makes the hackle look as though it is coming right out of the dubbing when it is wrapped.

An additional advantage of this method is that the hackle can be pulled to the sides more naturally after it has been wrapped. In other words, the hackle is less likely to need trimming so that the fly lays flatter on the water's surface. This hackling method can be used on a variety of emergers as well as standard dry flies. Besides saddle hackle I also like to use hen necks. Whiting's hen necks are great for this because the feathers are long and the stems are pretty small when compared to others. As you might guess, this type of hackling will create some of the most durable dry flies you will ever tie.

Step 1: About a 1/4 the way behind the hook eye, tie in some Z-lon and make sure that it extends beyond the end of the hook. Tie in a biot by the tip so that the notch is facing backward, then wrap it forward. The biot should end up in the thorax area. If the biot is too short, use micro tubing for the body.

Step 2: After the biot has been tied off, this is where the hackle is tied in. It helps if the hackle is tied in so that the exposed stem is tied in on the underside of the fly. Then place some Superfine dubbing onto your thread and wrap the thorax. Make sure to leave room behind the hook eye to tie off everything. As you do the thorax, make sure that the thread ends up where you tied in the hackle.

Step 3: Place a small amount of dubbing onto your thread. Wrap the hackle around your thread just like you would with peacock herl. Wrap it forward. Two or three turns are all that is needed.

Step 4: Then wrap it forward

Step 5: Take two or three CDC feathers and even up the tips. Tie them in so that the tips extend back towards the end of the body. This is like tying in the hair for an Elk Hair Caddis.

Step 6: Cut off the excess and tie off. Then pull the hackle fibers to the sides of the fly so that the fly will ride flush. If there are fibers that will not cooperate, just cut them off.

Bottom view.

Twisted Hackle Emerger, Gray

Hook:	Targus 2487 or equivalent, size 12-22
Thread:	Gray
Tail:	Gray Z-lon
Body:	Hareline's Premo goose biot gray dun
Wing:	CDC
Hackle:	Medium dun
Thorax:	Gray micro dry-fly dubbing

Twisted Hackle Emerger, Tan

Hook:	Targus 2487 or equivalent, size 12-22
Thread:	Tan
Tail:	Tan Z-lon
Body:	Hareline's Premo goose biot tan/dun
Wing:	CDC
Hackle:	Whiting's *Callibaetis* or equivalent
Thorax:	*Callibaetis* micro dry-fly dubbing

Twisted Hackle Emerger, Olive

Hook:	Targus 2487 or equivalent, size 12-22
Thread:	Olive
Tail:	Gray Z-lon
Body:	Hareline's Premo goose biot, Blue-Winged Olive
Wing:	CDC
Hackle:	Whiting's Blue-Winged Olive or equivalent
Thorax:	Blue-Winged Olive micro dry-fly dubbing

TOSHI KARITA

Stillborn Emerger

Hook:	Targus 2487 or equivalent, size 14-22
Shuck:	Z-lon or Ice Dub
Thread:	To match body color
Rear Gills:	Ostrich herl
Body:	Micro tubing
Thorax:	Micro dry-fly dubbing
Hackle:	Dry fly or soft hackle
Wing:	CDC

Once the mayfly reaches the surface, the transformation of the new fly is unveiled. The new insect wiggles and pulls itself free from its old body. As it does this, the head pokes out and then the wings follow. Sometimes the wings get trapped in the old skin, leaving them pressed against the body of the insect.

I've observed these insects on the water but it wasn't until my fishing buddy Mike Bostwick made some suggestions that I tied a fly incorporating this stage of the insect's life cycle. Curious how his idea might work, I sat down and tried to assemble his ideas. Our home waters are the South Platte and the Frying Pan River, where flies of this nature can make or break your day.

The key to this fly is to keep it fairly sparse looking. The body on the Stillborn Emerger is made of micro tubing but goose biot works just as well. The wings are tied in so that they resemble a mayfly stuck in its shuck, i.e., the wings haven't just pulled free of the shuck. To represent this your wings must lay along the side of the fly with just a hint of spread so that the fish can see them when it's viewed from the underside. CDC is perfect for this because of its natural medium-dun color, it floats pretty well and has a sheen to it because of its oils.

Since the wing is pulled backwards and tied off at the tail area, marabou, for the gills, is wrapped over it to help conceal where the wing was tied off. Also, once the wings have been tied in, trim off the excess. If you wish, you can leave some of the CDC so it lays over the top of the trailing shuck, adding a little more flotation to your fly. The key is to make sure that the wings loop outwards a little bit, giving the illusion of the stuck wings trying to pull free. Using the hackling methods already shown, you can choose whichever way you wish to hackle the thorax area. In this example, the twisted hackle method is used.

Since there is very little material sticking up or out of the fly, it will ride very low in the water, making it almost impossible to see as it floats down the river. To help you detect strikes, you can use a strike indicator, trail it behind a more visible dry fly or learn where your fly should be on the water after it is cast. There is no substitute for a well-presented fly and that only comes from practice. Lots of practice.

Step 1: Tie in the Z-lon for the shuck and then bring your thread forward to behind the hook eye.

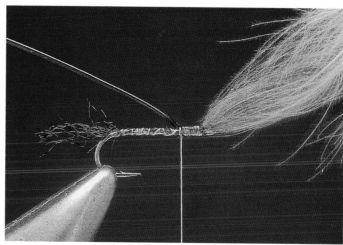

Step 2: Tie in two CDC feathers by the tips so that the excess is sticking out over the hook eye. Tie in the tubing right on top of the CDC.

Step 3: Tie in the hackle right behind the hook eye and then dub the thorax.

Step 4: Wrap the hackle backwards and tie it off at the back of the thorax, continue with the thread backwards until you get to the shuck. Wrap the tubing backwards as well and tie it off at the shuck area.

Step 5: Pull the CDC backwards and tie off at the shuck area. Make sure that the feathers fan out a little bit along the sides of the fly. Tie in a small amount of marabou by the tips. Twist it into a rope and take a couple of wraps and tie off.

Step 6: Pull the hackle to the sides of the fly so that it will ride flush. If any fibers are sticking out of the bottom, cut them off.

Top view.

Bottom view.

Stillborn Emerger, Gray

Hook:	Targus 2487 or equivalent, size 14-22
Thread:	Gray
Shuck:	Gray Z-lon
Gills:	Gray marabou
Body:	Gray micro tubing or small D-Rib
Wing:	CDC
Hackle:	Medium dun
Thorax:	Gray micro dry-fly dubbing

Stillborn Emerger, Tan

Hook:	Targus 2487 or equivalent, size 14-22
Thread:	Tan
Shuck:	Tan Z-lon
Gills:	Tan marabou
Body:	Tan micro tubing or small D-Rib
Wing:	CDC
Hackle:	Whiting's *Callibaetis* or equivalent
Thorax:	*Callibaetis* micro dry-fly dubbing

Stillborn Emerger, Olive

Hook:	Targus 2487 or equivalent, size 13-22
Thread:	Olive
Shuck:	Gray Z-lon
Gills:	Olive marabou
Body:	Olive micro tubing or small tubing
Wing:	CDC
Hackle:	Whiting's Blue-Winged Olive or equivalent
Thorax:	Blue-Winged Olive micro dry-fly dubbing

TOSHI KARITA

CDC Compara-Dun

Hook:	Targus 101 or equivalent, size 12-24
Thread:	Match the color of the body
Tail:	Mayfly tails
Body:	Hareline's Premo goose biots
Wing:	CDC
Veiling:	Mallard flank feather or partridge
Thorax:	Micro dry-fly dubbing

Before CDC, the Deer Hair Compara-dun was *the* fly for imitating small adult mayflies on selective trout waters. The wing and hackle is combined for an all-in-one approach. The splayed-out deer hair supports and floats the fly letting the fly ride flush on the water's surface. A new approach to designing adult flies without hackle. These flies "without hackle" can be said to have come from Doug Swisher's No-Hackles. Here, the duck quill wing fibers are the stabilizers and wings.

Dennis Black first introduced cul-de-canard to the American market in 1990 and the fun using these little feathers has yet to end. At the 20-year anniversary of the Federation of Fly Fishers in Eugene, Oregon, Ken Manard gave me some of these feathers. Not knowing what to do with them, but being told that they are great for floating flies, one of the first flies I used it on was the Compara-Dun. They were a godsend when compared to using deer hair for the wings. The wing tips can be used or fibers can be pulled from the stem and tied in clumps for the wing. Using the tips presents a clean finished fly but several feathers have to be used. Whether you are using the tips or the clump method, you can make your wing look a little different by using different colors of CDC when tying in your wing. For example, take two

white feathers to every gray feather used for a light dun color, or try using brown and gray feathers to form an Adams-colored wing.

Once the feathers are tied in, the most important thing to look for is CDC which has been pulled down onto the sides of the thorax. If after tying in the wing the fibers are not in place, all you have to do is pull the fibers down. To add a little pizzazz to your wing, tie in some mallard flank fibers (or wood duck) for a veiling effect in front of the wing. You can also add a trailing shuck. Just tie in some Z-lon, Antron, or Ice Dub before your body is made.

When adding floatant to the Compara-Dun, the CDC version requires a different approach. Since you don't want to matte down the fibers and remove the CDC's air-trapping qualities, a dry desiccant is best. I use Loon's Top Ride for the floatant and Easy Dry for reviving it after a fish is caught. Not meant for fast water, the CDC Compara-Dun does best on flatter water. If you feel a little creative streamside, try sinking this fly and fishing it as a drowned dun. This is especially effective at tailouts and within the riffles themselves. You can even turn it into an emerger by cutting the wing down.

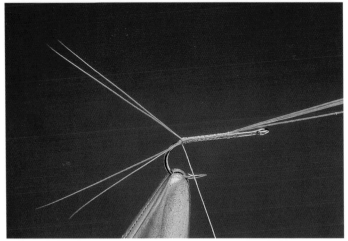

Step 1: Tie in four mayfly tails and figure-eight through them so that they are separated.

Step 2: Tie in a biot by the tip. With the notch facing backwards, wrap it forward. You should be about 1/3 the way back from the hook eye.

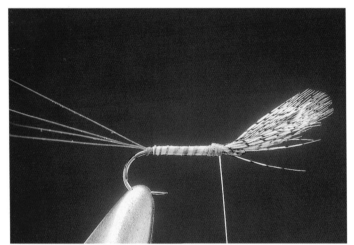

Step 3: Cut a "V" in the partridge. Tie in the partridge so that it extends the length of the body out over the hook eye. It should also be curving upwards.

Step 4: Take three to six CDC feathers and even up the tips. Tie them in so that they are the same length as the partridge. You can also tie in clumps of CDC in order to use the whole feather.

Step 5: Cut off the excess CDC and cover it with some dubbing. Pull the wing back and continue to dub in front of the wing. As you dub the head area, the wing should slant slightly back. Take off the thread. Pull down the CDC fibers along the sides of the thorax in order to form a semi circle on top of the hook.

Step 6: Front view.

Step 7: Same fly with a trailing shuck.

CDC Compara-Dun, Olive

Hook:	Targus 101 or equivalent, size 12-24
Thread:	Olive
Tail:	Medium dun mayfly tails
Body:	Hareline's Premo goose biot olive/dun
Wing:	CDC
Thorax:	Blue-Winged Olive micro dry-fly dubbing
Veiling:	Natural mallard flank

CDC Compara-Dun, Black

Hook:	Targus 101 or equivalent, size 12-24
Thread:	Black
Tail:	White mayfly tails
Body:	Black goose biot
Wing:	CDC
Thorax:	Black micro dry-fly dubbing

CDC Compara-Dun, Yellow

Hook:	Targus 101 or equivalent, size 12-24
Thread:	Yellow
Tail:	Yellow mayfly tails
Body:	Hareline's Premo goose biot, pale morning dun
Wing:	CDC
Thorax:	Pale Morning Dun micro dry-fly dubbing
Veiling:	Mallard flank dyed yellow

TOSHI KARITA

TOSHI KARITA

Medallion Dun

Hook:	Targus 101 or equivalent, size 14-22
Thread:	Match body color
Tail:	Mayfly tails
Body:	Hareline's Premo goose biots
Hackle:	CDC
Thorax:	Micro dry-fly dubbing
Wing:	Medallion sheeting or hen neck, (use Zing Wing for a spinner pattern)

Fly tiers tend to gravitate towards the tying methods of one tier or another. That tier for me was Rene Harrop. For years Rene and Bonnie have been producing an exquisite spinner pattern made from turkey flats. When Rene and I first started using CDC, he substituted it for their turkey flat wings. Z-lon added sparkle or translucency to the wing. After tying several hundred dozen of these flies, I thought, "Why not add upright wings to this spinner?" The spinner wings could be used as the hackle or legs. Around this time Medallion sheeting was produced so it was inevitable that it became my winging material of choice.

The wings are tied right on top or slightly in front of the spent wings so that when the dubbing for the thorax is added, it helps push the wings back into the right position (roughly 45° backwards). Most tiers don't have much trouble tying in the wings but find trimming them to be a challange. As I tell my students, envision the wings of a mayfly and trim your wing to that shape. To get a good idea of what the wings actually look like, I highly recommend *Hatches II* by Caucci and Nastasi. This book has pages filled with photos of insects which tiers can use as a reference. The key is to marry the wings together and pull them backwards. With the wings leaning towards the back, take one cut perpendicular to the hook shank and start at the bend of the hook. Then round off the corners to finish it off.

This is how I tied the first Medallion Dun, but I like to tinker around with things. For those tiers who cannot stand synthetic wings on their flies, a variation has been served up. After the fly is almost complete, except for the wing, dub in back of the thorax and around the wing to form the thorax. Then place a couple of hen neck wings in front of the legs and finish off the head.

The Medallion Dun rides flush on the surface and thus does not take well to riffles without becoming submerged. On windy days, or when using extremely small tippet, your leader can twist. Sometimes this twisting will happen and sometimes it won't, but one thing is for sure, the more you fish the Medallion Dun, the less likely this will happen. Having your wings slant back at an angle seems to be key in eliminating this problem. There are times when this twisting may be to your advantage because as the fly lands on the water, it will flip around, looking like a natural trying to free itself from the surface film.

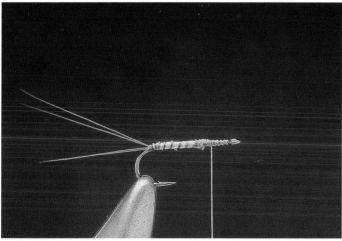

Step 1: Tie in four to six tails so that they are separated, with a series of figure-eights, into two equal groups. Tie in a biot by the tip, with the notch facing backwards, and wrap it forward. This should end up about 1/4 the way back from the hook eye.

Step 2: Take two to four CDC feathers and even up the tips. Tie them in with the tips sticking out over the hook eye at the same length as the body.

Step 3: Separate the feathers into two equal groups and figure-eight through them. It helps if you get at least one stem of the feather into each group. Also take several wraps of thread around the base of each feather to bring together any loose fibers.

Step 4: Cut a strip of the sheeting to the size of wing you want and tie it in just in front of or on top of the feathers.

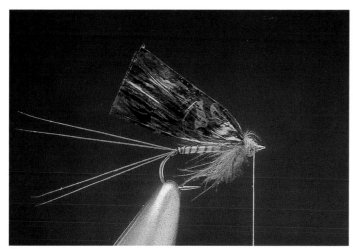

Step 5: Place some dubbing behind the wing then pull the wings and feathers back and continue with the dubbing in front of the wing. Dub onto the wing and feathers a little bit so that the wing slants backwards at an angle.

Step 6: Trim the wings to shape.

Step 7: Finished Medallion Dun.

Step 8: Shown with hen neck wings instead of Medallion sheeting.

Medallion Dun, Yellow

Hook:	Targus 101 or equivalent, size 14-22
Thread:	Yellow
Tail:	Mayfly tails, yellow
Body:	Hareline's Premo goose biot, pale morning dun
Wing:	Dun/yellow Medallion sheeting
Hackle:	White and gray CDC
Thorax:	Pale Morning Dun micro dry-fly dubbing

Medallion Dun, Olive

Hook:	Targus 101 or equivalent, size 14-22
Thread:	Olive
Tail:	Mayfly tails, dark dun
Body:	Hareline's Premo goose biot, olive/dun
Wing:	Medium dun Medallion sheeting
Hackle:	CDC
Thorax:	*Callibaetis* micro dry-fly dubbing

Medallion Dun, Adams

Hook:	Targus 101 or equivalent, size 14-22
Thread:	Gray
Tail:	Mayfly tail, dark dun
Body:	Hareline's Premo goose biot, gray dun
Wing:	Medium dun Medallion sheeting
Hackle:	Brown and gray CDC
Thorax:	Gray micro dry-fly dubbing

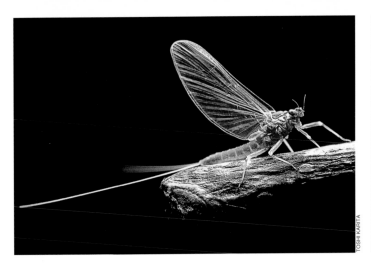

CDC Thorax Dun

Hook:	Targus 101 or equivalent, size 14-22
Thread:	Match body color
Tail:	Mayfly tails
Body:	Micro dry-fly dubbing.
Wing:	Hen hackle tips or turkey flats, (use Zing Wing for a spinner pattern)
Hackle:	CDC

Thorax dun refers to the point at which the hackle and wing are placed on the hook shank. This point would be in or near the middle of the hook shank. When Vince Marinaro first presented his ideas on this fly, he believed that a single upright wing (two feather tips put together) was sufficient to give the impression of a wing. Many tiers believe adult mayfly patterns need two wings separated into a "V" shape. The choice is yours. Both will work.

This particular pattern is meant to show, once again, that CDC can be used to replace the materials on some really good patterns. The hackle or leg section is made in the same manner as the Medallion Dun. The feathers are tied in spent, but this time it is done further down the hook shank. The wings are mounted in the middle of the spent feathers and posted so they stand upright. The body and thorax can be finished off with some dubbing. To give your wing a little more appeal to the fish, as well as your buddies, try using different colors of feathers for a mottled look.

This thorax-style fly is meant to ride more closely to the water's surface. Many who use the hackle version even cut a "V" in the bottom hackle so that the fly will ride almost flush to the surface. With the cost of hackle nowadays, why wrap all that hackle only to cut half of it away? By tying your thorax duns in the style shown, the need for cutting is eliminated and a few dollars are saved.

By using CDC though, your options for floating your fly are limited. Remember, any type of paste or liquid which mats down the fibers will destroy the floatability of the feathers. Once the fly is treated though, it is off to the water. If you are using no hackle, this fly is best used on those educated fish that live in clear, slow-moving waters. These educated fish relish the imprint this fly leaves on the water. The CDC fibers stick out from the sides and the middle of the body just like a natural. Flies tied up in this style have long been great imitations of Blue-Winged Olives, Pale Morning Duns and Mahogany Duns.

Step 1: Tie in two to four mayfly tails so that they are split into two equal groups.

Step 2: Take two to four CDC feathers and even up the tips. Tie them in the middle of the hook shank with the tips sticking out the front of the fly.

Step 3: Separate the CDC into two equal groups and figure-eight through them. Also take a few turns of thread around the base of each group to bring together all the loose fibers.

Step 4: Dub the body up to the hackle area and around the CDC.

Step 5: Tie in the wing right in front of the CDC and then continue to dub the rest of the body and head area.

Front view.

CDC Thorax Dun, Tan

Hook:	Targus 101 or equivalent, size 14-22
Thread:	Tan
Tails:	Tan mayfly tails
Body:	*Callibaetis* micro dry-fly dubbing
Wing:	Tan hen neck or turkey flat
Hackle:	Tan CDC

CDC Thorax Dun, Gray

Hook:	Targus 101 or equivalent, size 14-22
Thread:	Gray
Tail:	Dark dun mayfly tails
Body:	Gray micro dry-fly dubbing
Wing:	Gray hen neck or turkey flat

CDC Thorax Dun, Yellow

Hook:	Targus 101 or equivalent, size 14-22
Thread:	Yellow
Tail:	Yellow mayfly tails
Body:	Pale Morning Dun micro dry-fly dubbing
Wing:	Light dun hen neck or turkey flat

TOSHI KARITA

CDC Parachute Dun

Hook:	Targus 101 or equivalent, size 12-22
Thread:	Match the color of the body
Body:	Hareline's Premo goose biots
Wing:	Poly yarn
Hackle:	CDC
Thorax:	Micro dry-fly dubbing

Have you ever had one of those days when everything seems to be going wrong, then something finally goes right? That's what happened with this fly. There are very few, if any, new tying techniques but this fly *will* show you something new.

Parachute flies are one of the most widely used flies around. They are relatively easy to tie and, more importantly, they are easy to see on the water. Plus, when they are viewed from the underside (how all of your floating flies should be seen), its profile is a pretty close resemblance to the natural. The only problem with hackle parachutes is that the hackle has a hard time staying where you put it. Sure, glue can be used but it adds weight to the fly, plus an additional step in tying the thing. The CDC Parachute, however, resolves all these problems. The way in which this fly is tied makes the fly almost bombproof. Granted, you will probably

lose a few hairs from your own head out of frustration, but the more you practice, the easier it will get.

The key to the post is to use long-fiber material such as poly yarn, Z-lon, Antron, or even Zing Wing and Medallion sheeting. Poly is by far the easiest to use. It has a sufficient amount of compression, which the CDC fibers can bite into. The other materials will work but save them for another day when you have the technique down. The way in which the CDC is used in this fly lends itself nicely to almost any Parachute-type fly, including Blue-Winged Olives, Adams, Pale Morning Duns, and *Callibaetis*. For example, the Adams has a grizzly and brown hackle mixture so use a gray and brown. feather in its place. The results are the same, and the best part is your wallet is still full since you didn't have to buy two necks.

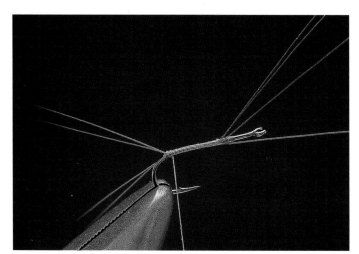

Step 1: Tie in four mayfly tails and separate them into two equal group by figure-eighting through them.

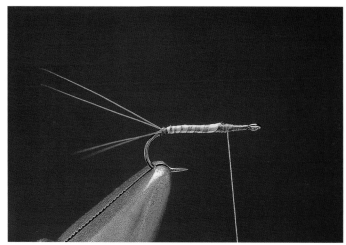

Step 2: Tie in a biot by the tip so that the notch is facing backwards. Wrap it forward.

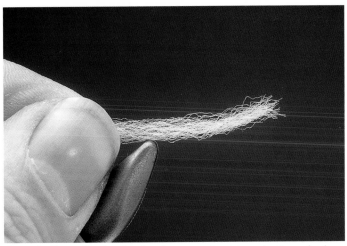

Step 3: Cut off a hunk of poly yarn about two to three inches. From that single rope, pull off roughly a 1/4 of it. This will be the post. The post will be doubled over so keep that in mind for your final post size.

Step 4: Take two feathers and even up the bases.

Step 5: Holding the feather tips in your right hand, pull the fibers back against the grain with your left hand. This will make the fibers stick out from the stem.

Step 6: Holding the feathers by the tips in your right hand, pull the fibers off the top of the feathers with your left hand.

Step 7: Then gently grab the bottom fibers with the same hand and with the previous fibers in them. You should now have a group of CDC fibers between your fingers.

Step 8: Grab the poly yarn in the middle and stick it into the middle of your CDC fiber bundle.

Step 9: Readjust the bundle if needed so that the poly stays on top of the CDC.

Step 10: Tie it down in the thorax with two turns of thread. Then take one turn of thread to form a figure-eight. The poly yarn should look like a spent wing on your hook.

Step 11: Reaching over the top of the wing and grabbing the fibers from the bottom and lifting up, take a very tight turn of thread around the base of the poly. Try to use only one turn of thread.

Step 12: Place some dubbing around the base of the wing and tie off.

Step 13: In one hand pull up on the poly wing, with the other hand grab the CDC and pull it straight down. While the. is pulled down cut it even with the hook point so that it's the length of the hook gap.

Finished CDC Parachute Dun.

Top view.

Bottom view.

CDC Parachute Dun, Tan

Hook:	Targus 101 or equivalent, size 12-22
Thread:	Tan
Tail:	Tan mayfly tails
Body:	Hareline's Premo goose biot tan dun
Post:	Poly yarn
Hackle:	Tan CDC
Thorax:	*Callibaetis* micro dry-fly dubbing

CDC Parachute Dun, Olive

Hook:	Targus 101 or equivalent, size 12-22
Thread:	Olive
Tail:	Dark dun mayfly tail
Body:	Hareline's Premo goose biot olive dun
Post:	Poly yarn
Hackle:	CDC
Thorax:	*Callibaetis* micro dry-fly dubbing

CDC Parachute Dun, Adams

Hook:	Targus 101 or equivalent, size 12-22
Thread:	Gray
Tail:	Dark dun mayfly tails
Body:	Hareline's Premo goose biot gray dun
Post:	Poly yarn
Hackle:	Brown and gray
Thorax:	Gray micro dry-fly dubbing

TOSHI KARITA

Medallion No Hackle

Hook:	Targus 101 or equivalent, size 14-22
Thread:	Match body
Tail:	Mayfly tails
Body:	Hareline's Premo goose biots
Wing:	Medallion sheeting,
	(use the clear sheeting for a spinner pattern)
Thorax:	Micro dry-fly dubbing

The No Hackle marks the beginning of when I first started to investigate flies, creating my own patterns. Mr. Swisher and Mr. Richard's book *Selective Trout* was a real eye-opener that got my juices going. In their book they have photos of naturals, as well as artificial flies, viewed from under water. As the old saying goes, a picture is worth a thousand words.

The hackled flies looked like a mess floating in the water totally obscuring the outline of the fly's body and hiding the wings. So, how come these flies have worked for all these years? Hackles are a necessary evil in order to float our flies, or are they? A few pages earlier I mentioned how the redistribution of the fly's weight is what helps it float and that is just what happens when the wings are mounted for the No Hackle. The wings stick out the sides of the thorax and transfer the weight along the fibers that are in contact with the water. Granted, flies of this nature will not survive a trip through the rapids but when fished over selective trout in smooth-flowing waters, the results can be eye-opening. Try fishing this fly during a hatch of Blue-Winged Olives, Pale Morning Duns, Tricos or *Callibaetis*.

The profile that the duck quill wings give this fly is impressive and very elegant, but can create a few hidden problems. For one thing, the correct type of duck quills should be used for both ease in tying and for the overall effectiveness of the fly. Not always an easy task. Then there is the problem of durability. If one is careful when removing the fly from the fish's mouth, the longevity of the wings is greatly increased. Although their stature will eventually diminish, the splitting of the wings does not mean the end of the fly's success.

Medallion sheeting helps with the wing mounting and provides a longer-lasting wing profile. When using duck quills, be careful not to split the wings before they are tied in. With Medallion sheeting, this problem is eliminated. If they are not tied in correctly the first time, just remove them and start over. Dubbing the thorax is when the simplicity of this fly really shows. With the sheeting in place for the wings, just push them forward out of your way as you dub behind the wings. Then pull the wings back into place as you finish off by dubbing the head area. This would not be so easy to do with duck quills.

The first thought that may have come to mind when you saw this fly was, I bet it will twist my leader. Well, to a certain extent you're right. If the wings are not leaning backwards at an angle, they can cause twisting. If you are a wild caster, it can twist your leader. If the wind is howling, this too can help in twisting your leader. If you are using light tippet, virtually any fly can twist your leader and this fly is no exception. One thing is for sure, though the longer you fish it, the better it gets.

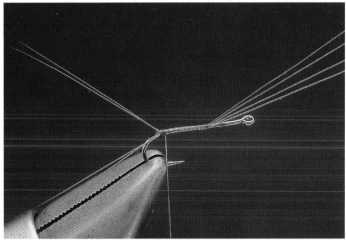

Step 1: Tie in two to four mayfly tails so that they are separated into two equal groups.

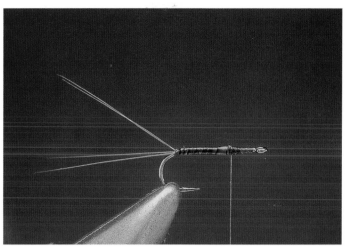

Step 2: Tie in a goose biot by its tip, with the notch in the biot facing backward.

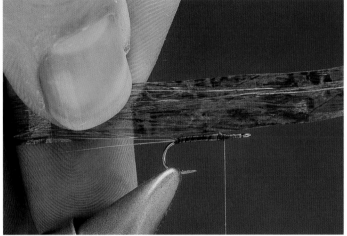

Step 3: Cut a strip of Medallion sheeting to the width of the wing you want.

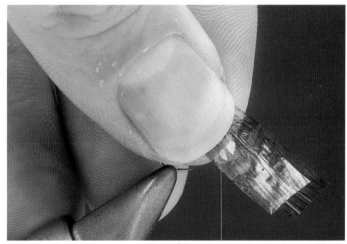

Step 4: Fold the sheeting in half and straddle the hook shank with it.

Step 5: With the thread between the sheeting, lift the thread straight up between the sheeting and then wrap the thread around the wing farthest from you and then one complete turn around both wings. This is all done with loose thread wraps and between your fingertips. Once the last complete turn of thread has been made, cinch down on the thread so that the wing is tied down to the hook shank. If you mess this up the first time, take the thread off and start over.

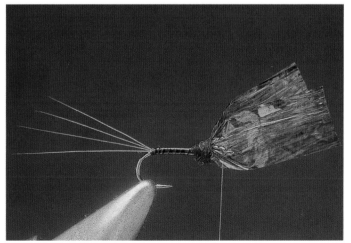

Step 6: Push the wings forward and then wrap some dubbing behind them.

Step 7: Pull the wings backwards and continue to dub in front of the wing, making sure that the wing is laying back at an angle. To get the wings to lay back, you might have to wrap some of the dubbing onto the front of the wing. Tie off the thread and then cut the wings to shape.

Finished Medallion No Hackle.

Bottom view.

Medallion No Hackle, Gray

Hook:	Targus 101 or equivalent, size 14-22
Thread:	Gray
Tail:	Dark dun mayfly tails
Body:	Hareline's Premo goose biot, gray dun
Wing:	Medium dun Medallion sheeting
Thorax:	Gray micro dry-fly dubbing

Medallion No Hackle, Black

Hook:	Targus 101 or equivalent, size 14-22
Thread:	Black
Tail:	White mayfly tails
Body:	Black goose biot
Wing:	Clear Medallion sheeting
Thorax:	Black micro dry-fly dubbing

Medallion No Hackle, Olive

Hook:	Targus 101 or equivalent, size 14-22
Thread:	Olive
Tail:	Dark dun mayfly tails
Body:	Hareline's Premo goose biot, Blue-Winged Olive
Wing:	Medium dun Medallion sheeting
Thorax:	*Callibaetis* micro dry-fly dubbing

TOSHI KARITA

Adult May

Hook:	Targus 101 or equivalent, size 14-22
Thread:	Match the body color
Tail:	Mayfly tails
Body:	Hareline's Premo goose biots
Hackle:	Dry fly
Thorax:	Micro dry-fly dubbing
Wings:	Medallion sheeting, (use clear for a spinner pattern)

The adult may is not meant to represent one specific hatch but rather most adult mayflies in general. Primarily, I like to use it for the Pale Morning Duns, *Callibaetis* and Blue-Winged Olives. The only differences in tying these three species is in the size of the hook used and the color of the materials. This fly is a knockoff of the old standard patterns, with some new materials.

For the tails, hackle barbs are substituted with mayfly tails (Micro Fibbetts) and goose biots replace the dubbed bodies. For wings, Medallion sheeting is used to form the most realistic wings. The split mayfly tails give the fly more stability in the water and the way in which they are tied in is also much easier than using the old dubbed-ball routine. The biot body is about as close as you can get to the natural body, short of peeling off the skin and trying to wrap that onto the hook. The wings can be shaped into any configuration you want and they also look very life-like.

The beauty of this fly is the ease with which it is tied. This is especially helpful when tying Blue-Winged Olives in a size 20 or smaller. The wings can be left long and then trimmed down to size which is nice for those who have less-than-nimble fingers. The biot can be grasped with hackle pliers and then wrapped forward. When the biot is wrapped forward, a natural taper is achieved along with natural-looking segmentations. The body that was once dubbed (usually with too much material) is now simplified with this little substitution.

The sheen that the wings give off, besides from looking natural, actually helps the angler follow the fly down the river. It is a great advantage if you see the fish take your offering instead of guessing that the rise was for your fly. To help it float even higher and longer, floatants can be added. If you plan ahead, the best floatant around is Water Shed. This relatively new product has to be placed on your fly 24 hours before you go fishing for the best results. If you have procrastinated though, the floatant of your choice will work streamside.

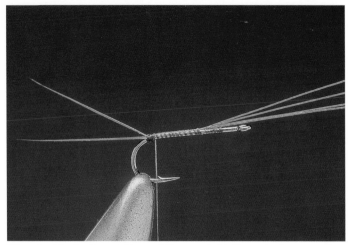

Step 1: Tie in four tails and figure-eight through them so that they are separated.

Step 2: Tie in a biot by the tip and with the notch facing backwards. Wrap it forward so that the body ends about 1/4 the way back from the hook eye.

Step 3: Tie in the hackle at the back of the thorax and a strip of the sheeting for the wings behind the hook eye. Then dub the thorax.

Step 4: Wrap the hackle through the thorax and up to the wings. Then wrap the thread back into the hackle.

Step 5: With the thread in the hackle, pull the wings straight back and tie them down. Make sure that the wings are slanted back at an angle. Tie off.

Finished Adult May.

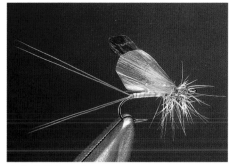

Adult May, Orange

Hook:	Targus 101 or equivalent, size 14-22
Thread:	Yellow
Tail:	Yellow mayfly tails
Body:	Hareline's Premo goose biot, Sulphur orange
Wing:	Dun yellow Medallion sheeting
Hackle:	Light dun
Thorax:	Sulphur orange micro dry-fly dubbing

Adult May, Tan

Hook:	Targus 101 or equivalent, size 14-22
Thread:	Tan
Tail:	Tan mayfly tails
Body:	Hareline's Premo goose biot, tan dun
Wing:	Tan Medallion sheeting
Hackle:	Whiting's *Callibaetis* or equivalent
Thorax:	*Callibaetis* micro dry-fly dubbing

Adult May, Adams

Hook:	Targus 101 or equivalent, size 14-22
Thread:	Gray
Tail:	Dark dun mayfly tail
Body:	Hareline's Premo goose biot, gray dun
Hackle:	Brown and grizzly
Thorax:	Gray micro dry-fly dubbing

TOSHI KARITA

Adult Green Drake

Hook:	Targus 2312 or equivalent, size 10-14
Tail:	Mayfly tails
Thread:	Match the body color
Body:	White single-strand floss. Color with Chartpak celery (light) or pale olive (darker)
Ribbing:	Pheasant tail micro tubing
Wing:	Medallion sheeting
Hackle:	Dry fly
Thorax:	Awesome Possum dubbing

The very first fly tying book I read was Terry Hellekson's book *Popular Fly Patterns*. In this book is a section on flies like no others I'd seen, the Water Walkers. Terry credits Frank Johnson for their development. Their unusual hackling is shown here. The hackle is wrapped around each wing like a parachute which creates a "V" in the hackle when viewed from the underside (the trout's view).

Since I try to incorporate as much realism into my flies as possible, this hackling technique soon became the best way to accomplish this. The problem with Green Drakes is that they are big. I mean really big. When you are used to tying on hooks that range in size from 16-24, the departure to something gigantic like a 10 or 12 is quite challenging. Trying to devise a way in which to float this fly is one thing, then you have to take into account where it will be fished. Since the Green Drakes in Colorado (on the Roaring Fork and Frying Pan) can be seen floating in riffles as well as slack water, a high-floating fly is almost a necessity. This is also true for both the Gray and Brown Drakes. This is when the Water Walker way of hackling came to mind (nearly 20-some years later). The wings of the natural are huge and to make the fly

look in proportion, the hackle would have to be just as big. The only problem with this is that when you add this much hackle to your fly and view it from the underside, you know that the fish are laughing at you for presenting such an offering. Yes, I know, these types of flies have been around for decades and have been proven producers, but remember I strive towards realism whenever possible.

With the Water Walker hackling method, which most have not even heard of, we once again take a technique from the past and incorporate it into our flies today. In this case it's using floss for the body. When in the vise, the floss body looks relatively realistic. When it gets wet, though, it looks totally different; The floss looks lifelike, or skin like. When coupled with rust-colored micro tubing for the ribbing, the end result is quite pleasing.

Because of their size, the wings of the natural are what most anglers see first because of their size. They extend back into the middle of the tail. In order to replicate this feature, mottled gray Medallion sheeting is used. The wings can be made as long and as wide as you want, they give a good base in which to wrap the hackle. Once all is in place, the end result is remarkably close to the natural when viewed from the underside.

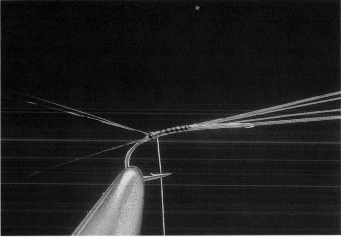

Step 1: Tie in six to eight tails and separate them with figure-eights so that they are in two equal groups.

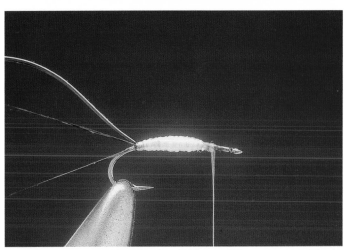

Step 2: Tie in the tubing for the ribbing and form a tapered body with the floss.

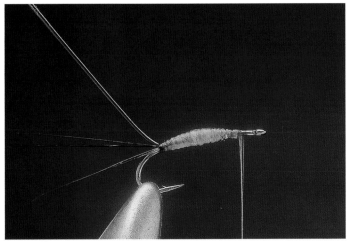

Step 3: Use a Chartpak marker to color the body. The more you go over the body, the darker it will get. So use your own judgment on how dark you want it.

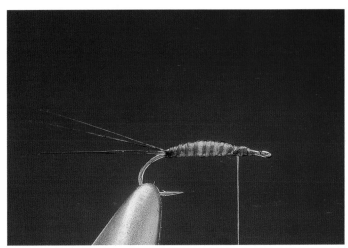

Step 4: Rib the body with the tubing. The body should be 1/4 the way back from the hook eye.

Step 5: Cut a strip of sheeting to the width you want your wings to be. Tie them in where you left off with the body.

Step 6: Take some dubbing and place a small amount behind the wing and then in front of it. Also, figure-eight around the wing once or twice. As you do this, make sure that the wings remain slanting back at an angle.

Step 7: Tie in two hackles with one at the base of each wing. Add a little more dubbing to cover up where you tied in the hackle. While doing this, do not crowd the head area.

Step 8: Wrap the hackle around the base of each wing and tie off.

Finished Adult Green Drake.

Bottom view.

Adult Green Drake, Brown Drake

Hook:	Targus 2312 or equivalent, size 10-14
Thread:	Brown
Tail:	Dark mayfly tails
Body:	White floss marked with mocha marker
Ribbing:	Micro tubing, brown
Wing:	Mottled brown Medallion sheeting
Hackle:	Whiting's March Brown or equivalent
Thorax:	Brown micro dry-fly dubbing

Adult Green Drake, Gray Drake

Hook:	Targus 2312 or equivalent, size 10-14
Thread:	Gray
Tail:	Dark dun mayfly tails
Body:	White floss marked with gray marker and a little tan
Ribbing:	Gray micro tubing
Wing:	Mottled gray Medallion sheeting
Hackle:	Grizzly dyed dun
Thorax:	Gray micro dry-fly dubbing

Adult Green Drake, March Brown

Hook:	Targus 2312 or equivalent, size 10-14
Thread:	Brown
Tail:	Dark mayfly tails
Body:	White floss marked with goldenrod marker
Ribbing:	Brown micro tubing
Wing:	Hopper tan Medallion sheeting
Hackle:	Whiting's March Brown or equivalent
Thorax:	Brown micro dry-fly dubbing

TOSHI KARITA

Winger Parachute

Hook:	Targus 101 or equivalent, size 12-22
Thread:	Match body color
Body:	Hairline's premo goose biots
Tail:	Mayfly tails
Wing:	Hen neck feathers
Hackle:	Dry fly
Thorax:	Micro dry-fly dubbing

Parachute-type flies are without a doubt the most popular dry flies. They are easy for the angler to see but, more importantly, the silhouette that this type of fly presents is very lifelike. When viewed from underneath, the fly's segmented body is more prevalent if you use a biot or some type of ribbing. The thorax area looks as if it has legs sticking out the sides, unlike a regularly hackled fly. These characteristics make it ideal for a Blue-Winged Olive or Pale Morning Dun hatch.

When we hear a fly referred to as a parachute, we generally visualize that the hackle has been wrapped around a post. For the most part, the post is made out of poly yarn, Z-lon, or calf tail. These types of posts have been used for decades and with great success. When we think of adult mayflies though, we visualize a tiny insect with upright wings. These last two sentences are what set me to thinking. Why aren't parachutes tied with wings? The experiments began and I settled on using hen hackle tips. Using hen necks for wings is nothing new, A.K. Best popularized them some time ago. However, using them for parachute wings is a little different.

The first problem I found was that the wings are somewhat flimsy, compared to a solid post, for wrapping the hackle around.

Adding some dubbing around the base of the wing and a turn in-between them to help separate them, proved invaluable. The dubbing gave the wings a base in which the hackle could grab onto and stay in place. The rest of the fly can be tied however you wish but this example uses a biot for the body.

The simple little step of placing some dubbing between the wings presents the fly in a much more natural way when viewed from the underside. This view shows the presence of wings something never before seen on a parachute mayfly. Just think of all the new flies that can be tied this way: Red Quills, Blue-Winged Olives, Pale Morning Duns and the list goes on. This is not a new technique but it shows how we can borrow ideas from other flies when we are tying our own. This is the beauty of fly tying, it allows us to be creative and personalize our flies.

A fly this delicate will naturally be more susceptible to injury but it holds its own pretty darn well. For better durability, and to help keep the wings spread, place a drop of glue between the wings. I like to soak these flies in Water Shed the night before I go fishing. That way, I will not have to treat them streamside. Once you get the hang of tying your parachutes this way, the old bulky calf tails will be put into a corner.

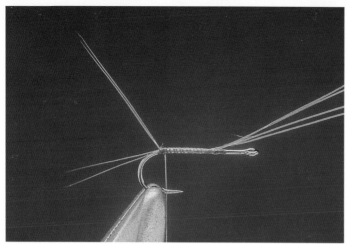

Step 1: Tie in the tails and figure-eight through them so that they are split.

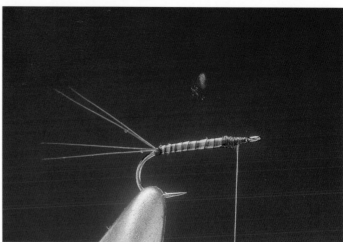

Step 2: Tie in a biot by the tip with the notch facing backward. Wrap it forward so that you end up about a 1/3 the way back from the hook eye.

Step 3: Tie the wings in the middle of the thorax.

Step 4: Dub around the base of the wing and then wrap some of the dubbing up the wing. Tie in the hackle.

Step 5: Wrap the hackle around the dubbed wing and tie off. As you wrap the hackle you might have to hold on to the wing as you make the wraps. If the wings are together, pull them apart and place a drop of glue between them to keep the wings divided.

Bottom view.

Top view.

Parachute Winger, Tan

Hook:	Targus 101 or equivalent, size 12-22
Thread:	Tan
Tail:	Tan mayfly tails
Body:	Hareline's Premo goose biot, tan dun
Wing:	Tan hen neck
Hackle:	Whiting's *Callibaetis* or equivalent
Thorax:	*Callibaetis* micro dry-fly dubbing

Parachute Winger, Olive

Hook:	Targus 101 or equivalent, size 12-22
Thread:	Olive
Tail:	Dark dun mayfly tails
Body:	Hareline's Premo goose biot, Blue-Winged Olive
Wing:	Medium dun hen neck
Hackle:	Whiting's Blue-Winged Olive or equivalent
Thorax:	*Callibaetis* micro dry-fly dubbing

Parachute Winger, Gray

Hook:	Targus 101 or equivalent, size 12-22
Thread:	Gray
Tail:	Dark dun mayfly tail
Body:	Hareline's Premo goose biot, gray dun
Wing:	Medium dun hen neck
Hackle:	Medium dun
Thorax:	Gray micro dry-fly dubbing

TOSHI KARITA

Compara May

Hook:	Targus 101 or equivalent, size 14-24
Tail:	Mayfly tails
Thread:	Match body color
Body:	Hareline's Premo goose biots
Wing:	Hen hackle tips. Use Zing Wing or clear Medallion sheeting for a spinner pattern
Hackle:	Dry fly
Thorax:	Micro dry-fly dubbing

When it comes to matching the hatch on spring-creek waters, the Compara May will fool the most weary of trout. The key to this fly lies in its design. The Compara-Dun has long been a staple in the arsenal of flies used by anglers fishing educated waters. This fly, however, takes that design one step further by adding wings.

When viewed from the underside, the outline of the wings of the natural is undisputed. It only makes sense to add this feature to any or all of your mayflies. The hackling is another feature which is somewhat new. The hackle fibers are pulled up from the underside so that the thread, which is pre-dubbed, can be figure-eighted underneath. This technique will pull up and hold the hackle fibers in position, eliminating the need for cutting the hackle from the bottom. This also relieves you from wasting part of your multi-dollar hackle.

The nice thing about using hackle in this form is that it can actually give the legs a mottled affect. I like to use Whiting's dun grizzly for this. They have a faint barring to them and the white portion of the feather can be dyed to whatever color you desire. Thinking of dying a $75 saddle or neck can bring a grown person to tears, but relax, it is probably easier than tying this fly. Get some Rit dye and a $2 loaf pan from the grocery store. Warm up some water in the pan and place a teaspoon of dye into

it for a test run. Pluck a feather and place it into the dye bath. If you like what you see, place the whole pelt in and you will be done in minutes. Dry the neck or saddle between some paper with some weight on it. If you don't add the weight, the neck will curl up when it dries. There are books available about dying materials, ask your favorite shop owner for some help. However, if you do not want to dye your own feathers, don't worry. Once again, Tom Whiting has gone that extra step. He just made available some new feathers designed to match some major hatches, including Pale Morning Duns, Blue-Winged Olives, *Callibaetis* and March Browns. At last, we have some hackle which actually looks like the natural's legs.

This is not a fly for fishing the rapids, as I am sure you can tell. Yet, for flat waters and fishing the edges of the seems, this fly may be just the ticket to a memorable afternoon on the water. I like to pre-soak mine with Water Shed the night before I go fishing, that way when I get to the water, I am already to go. Using any natural material, other than CDC, any floatant will work.

Hackling your fly with this technique will take some practice, so at first use old feathers you don't really care about. Once you get the hang of it, use the good stuff then sit back and enjoy the piece of work you just completed.

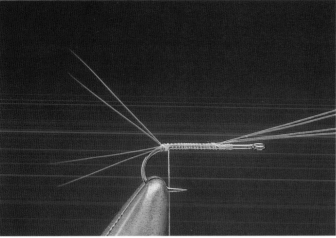

Step 1: Tie in the tails so that they are split by doing a figure-eight through them.

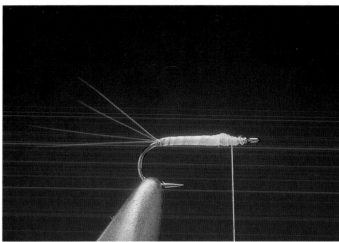

Step 2: Tie in a biot by the tip. With the notch facing backward, wrap it forward. You should be about 1/3 the way back from the hook eye.

Step 3: Tie in the hackle and then add a little bit of the dubbing to the thorax.

Step 4: Tie in the wings, then cover up where you tied in the wings with some more dubbing.

Step 5: Wrap the hackle forward with several turns. Make sure that you have room in front for a dubbed head.

Step 6: With the thread up by the hook eye, place more dubbing onto the thread. With your left hand, reach over the top of the fly and grab the hackle from the underside and pull it upwards. While the hackle is up, take the dubbed thread and take a turn of the thread underneath the fly and take a wrap behind the hackle. Pull the hackle up again, especially on the side away from you, and bring the thread back under the fly and up to the hook eye.

Step 7: Repeat this process a couple of times until all the hackle from under the fly is sticking out the sides of the thorax.

Step 8: You are basically performing figure-eights on the underside of the fly.

Step 9: It should form a hackle profile that's 180 degrees on top of the hook shank or look like a Compara-Dun wing.

Finished Compara May.

Front view.

Compara May, Tan

Hook:	Targus 101 or equivalent, size 14-24
Thread:	Tan
Tail:	Tan mayfly tails
Body:	Hareline's Premo goose biot, tan dun
Wing:	Tan hen neck
Hackle:	Whiting's *Callibaetis* or equivalent
Thorax:	*Callibaetis* micro dry-fly dubbing

Compara May, Olive

Hook:	Targus 101 or equivalent, size 14-24
Thread:	Olive
Tail:	Dark dun mayfly tail
Body:	Hareline's Premo goose biot, olive dun
Wing:	Medium dun hen neck
Hackle:	Whiting's Blue-Winged Olive or equivalent
Thorax:	*Callibaetis* micro dry-fly dubbing

Compara May, Gray

Hook:	Targus 101 or equivalent, size 14-24
Thread:	Gray
Tail:	Dark dun mayfly tails
Body:	Hareline's Premo goose biot, gray dun
Hackle:	Medium dun
Thorax:	Gray micro dry-fly dubbing

Extended May

Hook:	Targus 921 or equivalent, size 12-20
Thread:	Match body
Body:	Hareline's extended bodies
Hackle:	Dry fly or saddle
Wing:	Hen neck, (use Zing Wing or clear Medallion sheeting for a spinner pattern)
Thorax:	Micro dry-fly dubbing

Pre-formed bodies are something of a novelty in the fly-tying world. Who would of thought that one day we could purchase parts for our flies already made up? These little mayfly bodies eliminate the trouble of creating your own bodies. They are realistic, with split tails and glistening bodies complete with segmentations, ready to use for whichever hatch we may encounter. These hatches include Blue-Winged Olives, Pale Morning Duns, Red Quills and *Callibaetis*.

Take a body from the package and tie it onto a short-shank hook. Add some wings and hackle and you are done. To help keep it from spinning on the hook shank, lay a thread base down first and then after the body is tied down, put some Zap-a-Gap on it. For those who wish to spend more time at the vise, see the section on extended bodies starting on page 21.

White is the most versatile color. Because these bodies are made of synthetic materials they readily take magic markers. The fly shown represents a pretty conventional style of dry fly with its hackle and wings. But do not limit yourself to just this one style, try tying some with a parachute, a No-Hackle, or even a Compara-Dun. Besides being used for an adult pattern, these bodies lend themselves nicely to spinner patterns as well.

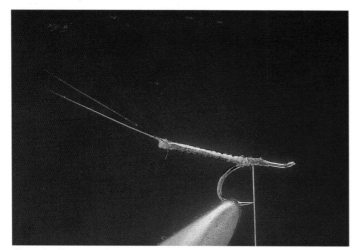

Step 1: Tie a pre-formed body onto the hook.

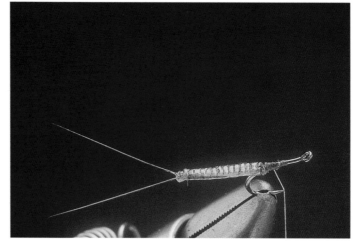

Top view.

Step 3: Tie in the wings in the middle of the hook shank. Also take a few turns of thread between the wings to keep them separated.

Step 4: Tie in the hackle and dub the rest of the hook shank.

Step 5: Wrap the hackle forward and tie off. This fly also lends itself nicely to a parachute.

Top view.

Extended May, Gray

Hook:	Targus 921 or equivalent, size 14-20
Thread:	Gray
Body:	Hareline's extended body, gray
Wing:	Gray hen neck
Hackle:	Medium dun
Thorax:	Gray micro dry-fly dubbing

Extended May, Tan

Hook:	Targus 921 or equivalent, size 14-20
Thread:	Tan
Body:	Hareline's extended bodies tan
Wing:	Tan hen neck
Hackle:	Whiting's *Callibaetis* or equivalent
Thorax:	Micro dry-fly dubbing *Callibaetis*

Extended May, Yellow

Hook:	Targus 921 or equivalent, size 14-20
Thread:	Yellow
Body:	Hareline's extended body, white then marked with yellow marker
Wing:	Light to medium dun hen neck
Hackle:	Whiting's Pale Morning Dun or equivalent
Thorax:	Micro dry-fly dubbing, Pale Morning Dun

TOSHI KARITA

Deer Dun

Hook:	Targus 2312 or equivalent, size 10-16
Thread:	Match body color
Tail:	Mayfly tails
Back strap:	Deer hair
Ribbing:	Tying thread
Thorax:	Micro dry-fly dubbing
Legs:	Deer hair the same as back strap
Wing:	Medallion sheeting

When it comes to dry flies, hackle has been the answer to floatation and the illusion of legs. However, hackle can be very expensive and the colors you want may not be available. My search for an alternative to hackle led to deer hair.

When you look at how a natural dun sits on the water's surface it becomes very clear why we often trim the hackle from the underside of our flies. The duns do not sit up out of the water, instead they sit flush on it. Using deer hair to redistribute the weight of the fly's body in place of the hackle seemed plausible in theory. The deer hair, or elk if you prefer, can be made into a post on the underside of the fly. With a push of the finger into the center, the pressure splays the fibers outward, just like the legs of a

natural. To hold them in place, a series of thread turns between the fibers is required and a little glue doesn't hurt either. The body and wings can be modified to use whatever materials you want.

This fly is not meant for fast water, however, when used on flat water, this low-riding fly can pick up the fussiest trout. Especially if they are used for the March Brown and *Callibaetis*. This fly will surprise you with how well it actually floats. The deer-hair fibers stick out the front of the fly, the middle of the thorax, and the back of the fly in a much more natural appearance than hackle. When is the last time you saw an insect's legs sticking straight out from its body, in a complete circle? This is why the deer-hair legs work so well.

Step 1: Tie in four to eight mayfly tails and split them into two equal groups.

Step 2: Tie in thread for ribbing and tie in deer hair for the back strap. It helps if after you tie in the hair, you continue to hold onto the tips so that you can trim them before they intermix with the tail fibers.

Step 3: Dub the body so that it tapers from the back towards the front of the fly. You should end up about a 1/4 the way back from the hook eye. Pull the deer hair over the top and tie it down. Then take your thread ribbing and rib the body. If you are using fine thread, take two turns of thread for each segment wrap.

Step 4: Cut a strip of Medallion sheeting to the width you wish your wings to be. Then tie it in right behind the hook eye. Cover up the thorax with a small amount of dubbing.

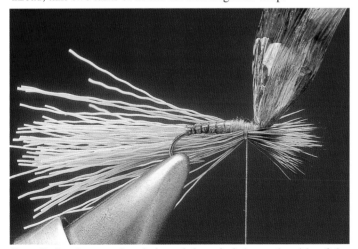

Step 5: Stack some deer hair and then tie it in on the side of the thorax, away from you, with the tips sticking out the front of the fly. As you tighten the thread the hair should roll to the underside of the fly where you want it. Cut off the excess hair and cover it with some dubbing.

Step 6: Pull some deer hair back and tie down at the back of the thorax. Pull the wings back and tie down with one turn of thread. In the same place, pull back some hair and tie down. Take the thread under the thorax to the hook eye and tie off. You are basically separating the hair so that it splays out like a parachute hackle with your thread. If you have any fibers sticking out the bottom, trim them off.

Finished Deer Dun.

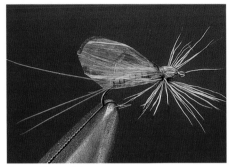

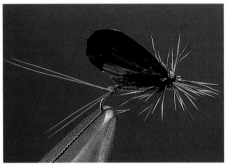

Deer Dun, Olive

Hook:	Targus 2312 or equivalent, size 10-16
Thread:	Olive
Tail:	Dark dun mayfly tails
Body:	Blue-Winged Olive micro dry-fly dubbing
Back Strap:	Olive deer hair
Ribbing:	Brown thread
Wing:	Medium dun Medallion sheeting
Legs:	Olive deer hair
Thorax:	Blue-Winged Olive micro dry-fly dubbing

Deer Dun, Tan

Hook:	Targus 2312 or equivalent, size 10-16
Thread:	Tan
Tail:	Tan mayfly tails
Body:	*Callibaetis* micro dry-fly dubbing
Back Strap:	Tan deer hair
Ribbing:	Brown thread
Wing:	Tan Medallion sheeting
Legs:	Tan deer hair
Thorax:	*Callibaetis* micro dry-fly dubbing

Deer Dun, Brown

Hook:	Targus 2312 or equivalent, size 10-16
Thread:	Brown
Body:	Brown micro dry-fly dubbing
Back Strap:	Brown deer hair
Ribbing:	Brown thread
Wing:	Brown Medallion sheeting
Legs:	Brown deer hair
Thorax:	Brown micro dry-fly dubbing

Soft Hackle Spinner

Hook:	Targus 101 or equivalent, size 14-24
Thread:	Match color of the body
Tail:	Mayfly tails
Body:	Hareline's Premo goose biots
Shellback:	Medallion sheeting
Wing:	Hen neck
Thorax:	Micro dry-fly dubbing
Hackle:	Hen neck

Once the mayfly transforms from adult to spinner, a new set of options arise for the tier. Unlike the adult's upright wings, the spinner's wings lie spent from the sides of the thorax. Another feature that distinguishes the spinner from the adult is the length of the tail. The spinner's tails are one and a half to two times the length of the body. The legs on some species are also frequently longer in length. The tier should take notice of these characteristics.

Generally, we don't think of hackles when we think of spinners. As noted, the length of the legs can greatly increase and we leave a definite imprint on the water's surface. Since legs are such a prominent feature, why have we left out the hackle for so many years? We want the imitation to ride flush on the surface and the hackle, if conventionally wrapped, would raise the fly off of the surface. But if you use soft hackle, the fibers will flatten out when they get wet and add some movement to the fly.

The tier could also use a figure-eight to bring the fibers from the bottom of the fly to the top, like the Compara may, where they can be neatly trimmed.

Using soft hackle for legs works great in conjunction with a soft-hackle wing. The wings are tied in, the hackle is wrapped with a few turns, and then a shellback can be pulled over the top to hold down the wings and leg fibers. The shellback makes your flies stand out from the crowd. The soft hackle also helps in the flotation of the fly. It's been said several times now but I will say it again, the fibers help to redistribute the weight of the fly and leave an imprint on the water's surface. This imprint is perfect for Blue-Winged Olives, Pale Morning Duns, *Callibaetis* and just about any other spinner.

An alternative to hen hackle for the wings is Zing Wing, which was popularized by John Betts. This wing is clear like the natural's and because it is so thin and non-rigid, it will not twist your leader, most of the time.

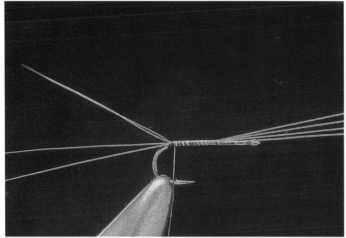

Step 1: Tie in three or four mayfly tail fibers so that they extend out at least 1 1/2 times the length of the body. To separate them, take a turn of thread around the underside of the tail so that it lifts them up a little bit.

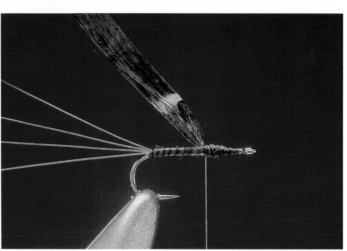

Step 2: Tie in a biot by the tip so that the notch is facing backwards. Wrap it forward. You should be about 1/3 the way back from the hook eye. Tie in the sheeting for the wing case.

Step 3: Tie in the hackle and then the wings. Figure-eight through the wings so that they lay spent.

Step 4: Figure-eight some dubbing around the wing and thorax area.

Step 5: Wrap the hackle forward with one turn behind the wing and two turns in front of the wing. Cut the hackle flat on top of the fly and then pull the wing case over the top and tie down and off.

Step 6: Pull the hackle fibers to the sides so that there is none on the bottom. If there are fibers sticking out the bottom, trim them off.

Top view.

Soft Hackle Spinner, Black

Hook:	Targus 101 or equivalent, size 14-24
Thread:	Black
Tail:	White mayfly tails
Body:	Black goose biot
Wing Case:	Dark dun Medallion sheeting
Wing:	White hen neck
Hackle:	Black
Thorax:	Black micro dry-fly dubbing

Soft Hackle Spinner, Yellow

Hook:	Targus 101 or equivalent, size 14-24
Thread:	Yellow
Tail:	Yellow mayfly tails
Body:	Hareline's Premo goose biot, pale morning dun
Wing Case:	Medium dun Medallion sheeting
Wing:	White or light dun hen neck
Hackle:	Whiting's Pale Morning Dun or equivalent
Thorax:	Pale morning dun micro dry-fly dubbing

Soft Hackle Spinner, Tan

Hook:	Targus 101 or equivalent, size 14-24
Thread:	Tan
Tail:	Tan mayfly tail
Body:	Hareline's Premo goose biot, tan dun
Wing Case:	Tan Medallion sheeting
Wing:	Tan hen neck
Hackle:	Whiting's *Callibaetis* or equivalent
Thorax:	*Callibaetis* micro dry-fly dubbing

JIM SCHOLLMEYER

Deer Spinner

Hook:	Targus 101 or equivalent, size 10-18
Thread:	Color to match body
Tail:	Mayfly tails
Body:	Hareline's Premo goose biots
Shellback:	Medallion sheeting
Legs:	Deer hair
Thorax:	Micro dry-fly dubbing
Wing:	Zing Wing

Using deer hair to replace hackle is once again explored in this spinner pattern. The only difference between this fly and the Soft-Hackle Spinner is the deer hair for the legs. As mentioned in the previous spinner, the legs of the natural can increase in length and they leave an imprint on the water's surface. Tying in this feature may just be what helps your fly stand out from the rest.

The deer-hair fibers work perfectly for legs because they taper from the base of the hair to the tip, and the tip of the hair is somewhat mottled. This is the most used portion of the hair in this application . If you look at the legs of a natural, they are usually not a solid color but rather barred or different shades of the base color, this makes these mottled tips very useful.

For wings, you can use hen hackle, Z-lon, Zing Wing, or whatever your heart desires. I am partial to Zing Wing so that is what I am using. As for the body, biots work wonders to form a segmented and tapered body, as does micro tubing ribbed with FisHair. Some say that the tubing is too heavy but not when compared to a water-logged dubbed body. And since the tubing is hollow it will naturally trap air, aiding in floatation and giving the body a nice wet sheen.

Fishing spinners is not easy. For the most part, you will not be able to see your fly on the water as it is flush with the surface. Then how can you tell if a fish has taken your offering? Know where your fly is at all times. That means pick out a fish and cast to it. Cast upstream or downstream for the best drag-free drift. Once your fly lands on the water, you should be able to tell where it is by gauging how fast the water is moving between you and the fish. If you see a rise in the area of your fly, set the hook. More times than not, the fish is being cooperative and will take your fly.

Step 1: Tie in the mayfly tails so that they are semi split by placing one turn of thread under them. This will lift them and separate them somewhat.

Step 2: Tie in a biot by the tip so that the notch is facing backward and then wrap it forward. The biot should end up about 1/3 the way back from the hook eye.

Step 3: Cut a thin piece of Medallion sheeting for the wing case and then tie it in where you left off with the biot. Stack a small amount of deer hair and then tie it in with the tips towards the front. When tying in the deer hair start on the side of the hook shank away from you so that when you tighten the thread it will roll to the underside of the thorax. Cut off the excess hair.

Step 4: Cut a strip of Zing Wing to the width you want for your wings. Tie in the Zing Wing with two figure-eights and then pull on each end of the wing. This will straighten them out. Place some dubbing around the wing and thorax and have the thread end up just behind the wing.

Step 5: You can trim the wings now if you wish before the legs are in place. Pull some deer hair back on the side away from you and take one turn of thread around it. Do the same thing on the side towards you. Pull more hair back and take a turn of thread in front of it on each side of the hook so that the fibers stick out the side of the thorax. Then move the thread to the hook eye. As you move forward with the thread from the back to the front, you are basically wrapping the thread through the hair so that it splays out and becomes separated.

Step 6: Pull the wing case over the top and tie off. Turn the fly over and trim off any stray fibers. If you would like to stiffen up the hair fibers just place some head cement on them.

Bottom view.

Deer Spinner, Tan

Hook:	Targus 101 or equivalent, size 10-18
Thread:	Tan
Tail:	Tan mayfly tails
Body:	Hareline's Premo goose biot, tan dun
Wing Case:	Tan Medallion sheeting
Wing:	Tan Medallion sheeting
Legs:	Tan deer hair
Thorax:	*Callibaetis* micro dry-fly dubbing

Deer Spinner, Olive

Hook:	Targus 101 or equivalent, size 10-18
Thread:	Olive
Tail:	Dark dun mayfly tails
Body:	Hareline's Premo goose biot, Blue-Winged Olive
Wing Case:	Medium dun Medallion sheeting
Wing:	Medium dun Medallion sheeting
Legs:	Olive deer hair
Thorax:	*Callibaetis* micro dry-fly dubbing

Deer Spinner, Yellow

Hook:	Targus 101 or equivalent, size 10-18
Thread:	Yellow
Tail:	Yellow mayfly tails
Body:	Hareline's Premo goose biot, Pale Morning Dun
Wing Case:	Medium dun Medallion sheeting
Wing:	Clear Medallion sheeting
Legs:	Yellow or natural deer hair
Thorax:	Pale Morning Dun micro dry-fly dubbing

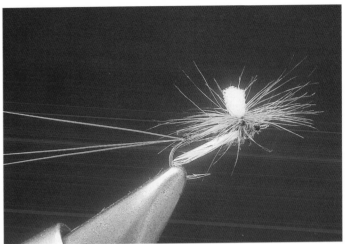

Parachute Spinner

Hook:	Targus 101 or equivalent, size 12-24
Thread:	Match body color
Tail:	Mayfly tails
Body:	Hairline's premo goose biots
Post:	Foam
Hackle:	Dry fly
Wing:	Zing Wing
Thorax:	Micro dry-fly dubbing

One of the greatest hatches to fish is a mayfly spinner fall. The only problem is that generally this hatch occurs towards dusk. As the light falls, so does our awareness of our fly. Aside from perfecting your casts, using a parachute greatly increases the presence of your fly. You can use parachutes for virtually every type of fly that you fish dry so it makes sense to do the same thing with spinners.

Any spinner pattern can be made into a parachute. This example is tied like the Soft Hackle Spinner with this one addition. When Zing Wing is used for the wings, the hackle will actually show through, giving the wings added venation and light coloring. Tie one and hold it up to the light to see what it looks like when viewed from underneath. Since the legs of the natural tend to increase in size during this molt, I like to use one hackle size bigger than I normally use. This way I not only get the added venation of the wings but also some nice-looking legs.

Using a thin strip of foam for the post works wonders. It has minimal build-up at the tie-in point and, most of all, it is very visible under low-light conditions. Once the hackle is wrapped, the post can be cut short if you wish, and the dilemma of the hackle coming off doesn't warrant a second thought. Since the hackle is wrapped on top of the fly via the parachute, the fly will ride flush on the surface and the overall flotation of the fly is greatly increased.

Step 1: Tie in the tails and then figure-eight through them so that they are separated.

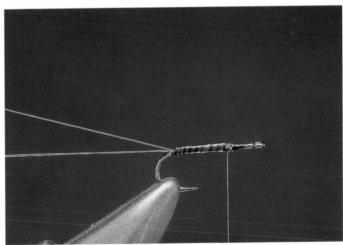

Step 2: Tie in a biot by the tip so that the notch is facing backward. Wrap the biot forward so that you end up about a 1/3 the way back from the hook eye.

Step 3: In the middle of the thorax, tie in a piece of foam and prop it up with your thread.

Step 4: Put some dubbing around the base of the post and then tie in the hackle and wings.

Step 5: Pull the wings back and finish dubbing in front of them.

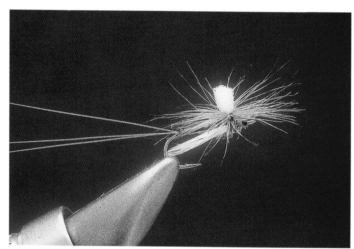

Step 6: Wrap the hackle around the post and tie off. A couple of turns is all that is needed for this fly.

Top view.

Bottom view.

Parachute Spinner, Yellow

Hook:	Targus 101 or equivalent, size 10-24
Thread:	Yellow
Tail:	Yellow mayfly tails
Body:	Hareline's Premo goose biot, Pale Morning Dun
Wing:	Zing Wing
Post:	Foam
Thorax:	Pale Morning Dun micro dry-fly dubbing
Hackle:	Whiting's Pale Morning Dun or equivalent

Parachute Spinner, Tan

Hook:	Targus 101 or equivalent, size 10-24
Thread:	Tan
Tail:	Tan mayfly tails
Body:	Hareline's Premo goose biot, tan dun or *Callibaetis*
Wing:	Zing Wing
Post:	Foam
Thorax:	*Callibaetis* micro dry-fly dubbing
Hackle:	Whiting's *Callibaetis* or equivalent

Parachute Spinner, Black

Hook:	Targus 101 or equivalent, size 10-24
Thread:	Black
Tail:	White mayfly tails
Body:	Black goose biot
Wing:	Zing Wing or clear Medallion sheeting
Post:	Foam
Thorax:	Black micro dry-fly dubbing
Hackle:	Black or grizzly dyed dun

Chapter 6

CRIPPLES

TOSHI KARITA

Emergent Cripple

Hook:	Targus 2487 or equivalent, size 12-22
Thread:	Match body color
Tail:	Soft hackle
Body:	Micro tubing
Ribbing:	FisHair
Underwing:	CDC
Wing:	Medallion sheeting
Thorax:	Micro dry-fly dubbing
Hackle:	Dry fly

When curved hooks came onto the scene new patterns using them sprang up like wildflowers. When it comes to emergers and cripples, the curved hook is very useful. The idea behind using the curved hook for emergers comes from wanting the butt of the fly to sink below the thorax and the wing portion makes it look as though the fly's crawling out onto the surface. Depending on what tailing material and floatant you use you can achieve this. However, if floatant is placed on the tail area and it is fairly stiff, it results in a fly which rides on its side.

Keeping this in mind, it is very important not to place floatant on the body of the fly and to use soft tailing and shuck materials. For this fly, the tail is made of partridge but any soft-hackle fibers will do. Since I want the body to ride below the thorax, I use D-Rib. The translucency is eye-catching and it develops a segmented body.

At first glance, this fly resembles the Loop Wing Emerger with its looped CDC underwing. The hackle allows the fly to ride a little higher on the surface as if it just crawled out onto it, and the wings present another stage of the insect's development. So that the fly does not roll over on its side, it is a necessity to trim a "V" in the bottom of the hackle so that the fly rides correctly. If you don't have CDC, Ice Dubbing works pretty well for the loop wing. Pull fibers from the package and tie in the tips. Once this is done, form a loop and tie it off. The reflective quality is something that natural materials just can't exhibit.

While on a trip to a favorite lake, it became evident that the birds were equally impressed with the fly. It was hard casting to a targeted fish because the birds just would not leave the Emergent Cripple alone. I figured if it could fool the birds, it would be no trouble fooling a few fish. It was a keeper.

Step 1: Tie in the tail, then cut the tubing at an angle and tie it in. Tie in some FisHair for the ribbing. Wrap the tubing forward and then the ribbing so that it goes in between the tubing. The body should be about 1/3 the way back from the eye.

Step 2: Tie in two CDC feathers by their tips so that the feather curves upwards. Tie in the hackle, and then the wings, behind the hook eye.

Step 3: Dub the thorax with a small amount of dubbing and then wrap the hackle forward. You should only need about two to three turns of the hackle. Cut the hackle flat on top and then form a loop in the CDC over the thorax and tie it down.

Step 4: Pull the wings along the sides of the thorax and tie them down. On larger-sized flies, you can also dub the head as shown. Trim and shape the wings. Pull the hackle fibers from the underside upwards so that there are very few, if any, fibers on the underside of the thorax. If you have fibers sticking out, cut them off.

Emergent Cripple, Tan

Hook:	Targus 2487 or equivalent, size 12-22
Thread:	Tan
Tail:	Soft hackle, partridge or Z-lon
Body:	Tan micro tubing
Underwing:	CDC
Wing:	Tan Medallion sheeting
Thorax:	*Callibaetis* micro dry-fly dubbing
Hackle:	Whiting's *Callibaetis* or equivalent

Emergent Cripple, Gray

Hook:	Targus 2487 or equivalent, size 12-22
Thread:	Gray
Tail:	Gray soft hackle, partridge or Z-lon
Body:	Gray micro tubing
Underwing:	CDC
Wing:	Medium dun Medallion sheeting
Thorax:	Gray micro dry-fly dubbing
Hackle:	Medium dun

Emergent Cripple, Rust

Hook:	Targus 2487 or equivalent, size 12-22
Thread:	Yellow
Tail:	Brown soft hackle, partridge or Z-lon
Body:	Rust micro tubing
Underwing:	CDC
Wing:	Dun yellow Medallion sheeting
Thorax:	Pale Morning Dun micro dry-fly dubbing
Hackle:	Whiting's Pale Morning Dun or equivalent

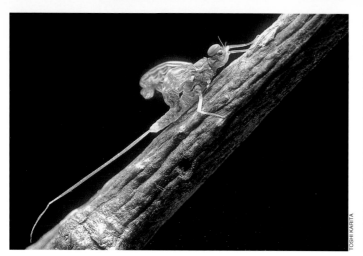

Emergent Cripple Dun

Hook:	Targus 2487 or equivalent, size 12-22
Thread:	Match body color
Tail:	Z-lon
Body:	D-Rib
Thorax:	Ice Dubbing
Hackle:	Hen neck or dry fly
UnderWing:	Ice Dubbing
Wing:	Medallion sheeting
Head:	Ice Dubbing

Not all mayflies reach the surface, escape from their shuck, and instantly transform into an adult. Sometimes the insect becomes crippled, giving the trout a little something different to look at. At times this is all that is needed to invoke a strike.

One of the best ways to tie a fly that is out of the ordinary is to use a curved hook. Depending on how you dress it, it will ride on the surface differently almost every time you cast it. You can use stiff hackle for the flotation, completely immerse your fly in floatant, or cast your fly into and below the surface.

This fly is meant to ride low on the surface with its abdomen hanging down below the thorax. To do this, the body is made of D-Rib which is not hollow. This will make the body heavier and more likely to sink. This works even better if you keep your floatant off of it. The hackle sticks out the sides of the thorax and not from the bottom. This can be done as you did with the Compara May or it can be trimmed off. By doing this, the fly is better at riding flush.

Adding Ice Dubbing for an underwing adds a little flash that attracts fish and also helps the angler see it. This fine, reflective material goes a long way so don't overuse it in your underwing.

When fishing over extra-selective trout, I like to trail this fly behind a more visible adult pattern. This way the fish is less likely to be spooked, and the end result is you removing your fly from the fish's mouth.

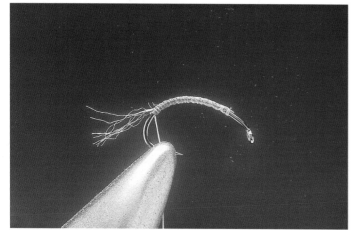

Step 1: Starting at the thorax, tie in several fibers of Z-lon for the shuck. As you wrap the thread back, pull straight back on the Z-lon as you tie it down.

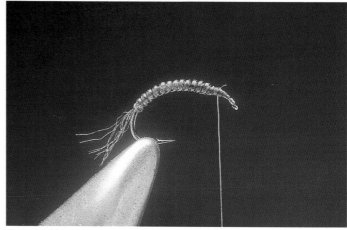

Step 2: Cut some D-Rib at an angle and tie it in by the tip. Wrap it forward to about 1/4 the way back from the hook eye.

Step 3: Tie in the hackle and dub the thorax. Do not crowd the head area as you will need room to tie in the wing and underwing.

Step 4: Wrap the hackle through the thorax and then trim it flat on top. Tie in the underwing and wing.

Step 5: Pull the wings back along the side of the thorax and tie them down. This can be done one wing at a time or both at the same time. Then dub the head.

Step 6: Trim the wings.

Emergent Cripple Dun, Tan

Hook:	Targus 2487 or equivalent, size 12-22
Thread:	Tan
Shuck:	Tan Z-lon
Body:	Tan small D-Rib
Hackle:	Whiting's *Callibaetis* hen or dry fly, or equivalent
Thorax:	UV tan Ice Dubbing
Underwing:	UV tan Ice Dubbing
Wing:	Tan Medallion sheeting
Head:	UV tan Ice Dubbing

Emergent Cripple Dun, Rust

Hook:	Targus 2487 or equivalent, size 12-22
Thread:	Yellow
Shuck:	Rust Z-lon
Body:	Rust small D-Rib
Thorax:	UV yellow Ice Dubbing
Hackle:	Whiting's Pale Morning Dun hen or dry fly, or equivalent
Underwing:	UV yellow Ice Dubbing
Wing:	Yellow dun Medallion sheeting
Head:	UV yellow Ice Dubbing

Emergent Cripple Dun, Brown

Hook:	Targus 2487 or equivalent, size 12-22
Thread:	Brown
Shuck:	Tan or medium brown Z-lon
Body:	Brown small D-Rib
Thorax:	UV brown Ice Dubbing
Hackle:	Brown hen or dry fly
Underwing:	UV brown Ice Dubbing
Wing:	Brown or mottled brown Medallion sheeting
Head:	UV brown Ice Dubbing

TOSH KARITA

Crippled Emerger

Hook:	Targus 101 or equivalent, size 14-22
Thread:	Match body color
Tail:	Mayfly tails crimped
Body:	Micro tubing
Ribbing:	FisHair
Underwing:	Ice Dubbing
Wing:	Medallion sheeting
Hackle:	Hen neck
Thorax:	Micro dry-fly dubbing

More and more people are hitting the water to pursue the finned prey. This abundance of pressure on the fish has educated the fish, giving the angler more of a challenge both on the water and at the vise. For some time now, we've heard of emergers and cripples. Cripples are injured insects singled out as easy prey. If you watch the National Geographic specials, the big cats almost always search for the injured or weakest animal in the herd. Trout are no different.

A crippled emerger also signals the dinner bell. When you see duns on the water and the fish seem to form a bowl in the surface, chances are they are feeding on helpless insects. This is when the Crippled Emerger is perfect. On spring creeks and tough rivers such as the South Platte, the fish have become so wary to our offerings anglers must try something else.

The tails of an injured mayfly aren't always straight or form a perfect "V". Using hemostats on the tails almost instantly forms an injured pattern. The tails become kinked and bent out of shape. The body can be made however you wish but make the wings look unnatural, such as one wing on top of the fly and the other sticking out the side. Adding soft hackle for legs adds to this crippled stage.

This fly is meant to be fished on or in the surface so the take is hard to see. A great way to fish this, or any emerger, is to trail it behind a more visible dun pattern. Once the dun has been pulled under, the hook can be set. You could also use an indicator on your leader or even use one of the specialized fly lines with built-in indicators. Just remember that this fly represents an injured insect so if you don't have this pattern while on the water, take any emerger in your box and mangle it up a little bit.

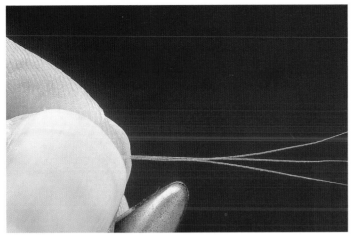

Step 1: Take three mayfly tails and squeeze them in a pair of hemostats.

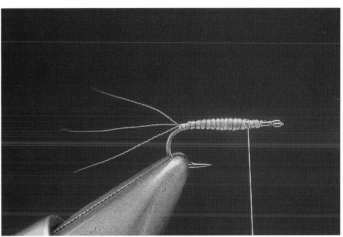

Step 2: Tie the tails in and figure-eight through them so that they become separated. Tie in a strand of FisHair for the ribbing. Cut some micro tubing at an angle and tie it in by the tip. Wrap the tubing forward and then follow it with the FisHair. Make sure the ribbing goes between the tubing segments. The body should end about a 1/3 the way back from the hook eye.

Step 3: Tie in a small amount of Ice Dubbing for an underwing where the body left off. Then tie in a hackle. Right behind the hook eye, tie in the Medallion sheeting wings.

Step 4: Place some dubbing in the thorax and then wrap the hackle forward. It will only need two or three turns of hackle. Wrap the thread backwards so that it ends up in the middle of the hackle.

Step 5: Pull the wings back and tie down. One wing should be on top of the fly and the other should be along the side. Remember you are tying a cripple. Tie off.

Step 6: Trim the underwing so that it's short of the end of the body, and then do the same thing with the wings. Pull the hackle to the sides of the fly so that very few fibers are sticking out the bottom of the fly. If there are hackle fibers on the bottom, trim them off. To make the wings look more crippled, grab them with your fingernails and pull them through it. This will give the wings a curved effect.

Crippled Emerger, Olive

Hook:	Targus 101 or equivalent, size 14-22
Thread:	Olive
Tail:	Dark dun mayfly tails crimped
Body:	Olive micro tubing
Ribbing:	Brown or olive FisHair
Underwing:	UV olive Ice Dubbing
Wing:	Medium dun Medallion sheeting
Hackle:	Whiting's Blue-Winged Olive or equivalent
Thorax:	*Callibaetis* micro dry-fly dubbing

Crippled Emerger, Yellow

Hook:	Targus 101 or equivalent, size 14-22
Thread:	Yellow
Tail:	Yellow mayfly tails crimped
Body:	Yellow micro tubing
Ribbing:	Olive FisHair
Underwing:	UV yellow Ice Dubbing
Wing:	Dun yellow Medallion sheeting
Hackle:	Whiting's Pale Morning Dun or equivalent
Thorax:	Pale Morning Dun micro dry-fly dubbing

Crippled Emerger, Gray

Hook:	Targus 101 or equivalent, size 14-22
Thread:	Gray
Tail:	Dark dun mayfly tails crimped
Body:	Gray micro tubing
Ribbing:	Black FisHair
Underwing:	UV gray Ice Dubbing
Wing:	Medium dun Medallion sheeting
Hackle:	Medium dun
Thorax:	Gray micro dry-fly dubbing

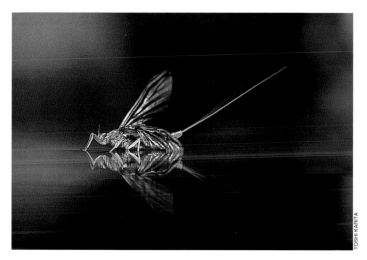

Crippled Dun

Hook:	Targus 101 or equivalent, size 14-22
Thread:	Match the body color
Tail:	Crimped mayfly tails
Body:	Hareline's Premo goose biots
Wing:	Zing Wing
Thorax:	Micro dry-fly dubbing
Hackle:	Dry fly or soft hackle

A newly-hatched dun emerges on the surface and begins to flap its wings in order to dry them so it can take flight. However, sometimes one wing might flap a little too hard and touch the water. The wing either gets trapped on the surface or the wing gets bent out of shape. Even more common, especially out West, the wind blows the insect over. All of these factors can create a crippled dun.

While at the vise, remember these scenarios when you start adding materials to the hook. The tails are crimped in a pair of hemostats, the body is whatever you desire, and the wings should reflect the dun fighting for its life. One of the best materials for this is Zing Wing, Mr. Betts' new-found material is perfect for imitating injured wings. It's translucent and after several casts it will begin to tear lengthwise, giving the illusion of an even more banged up fly.

As with emergers, you will probably have a tough time following this fly down river because it rides so low. Again, tie on a more visible dun pattern as your lead fly and trail this one behind it. If you are on flat water, this type of set-up is probably not needed. Since we are talking about a dun pattern, floatant is highly advised. One of the best places to try a crippled dun is where riffles turn into a flat run.

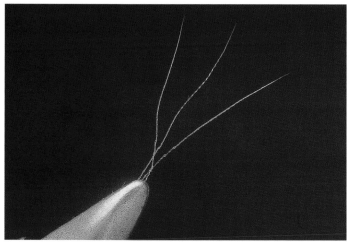

Step 1: Crimp three mayfly tails in hemostats and tie them in so that they are separated.

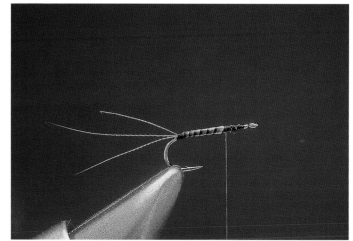

Step 2: Tie in the biot by the tip and with the notch facing backward. Wrap the biot forward. The body should be 1/3 the way back from the hook eye.

Step 3: Tie in the hackle and then tie in the wings right behind the hook eye. Dub the thorax.

Step 4: Wrap the hackle forward and tie it off. Then wrap the thread backward into the hackle and pull the wings back and tie down. Make sure one wing stands straight up on top of the fly and the other one is along the side of the thorax.

Front view.

Top view.

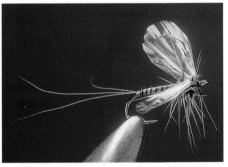

Crippled Dun, Tan

Hook:	Targus 101 or equivalent, size 14-22
Thread:	Tan
Tail:	Tan mayfly tails crimped
Body:	Hareline's Premo goose biot,, tan dun
Wing:	Zing Wing
Hackle:	Whiting's *Callibaetis* or equivalent
Thorax:	*Callibaetis* micro dry-fly dubbing

Crippled Dun, Yellow

Hook:	Targus 101 or equivalent, size 14-22
Thread:	Yellow
Tail:	Yellow mayfly tails crimped
Body:	Hareline's Premo goose biot, Pale Morning Dun
Wing:	Zing Wing
Hackle:	Whiting's Pale Morning Dun or equivalent
Thorax:	Pale Morning Dun micro dry-fly dubbing

Crippled Dun, Olive

Hook:	Targus 101 or equivalent, size 14-22
Thread:	Olive
Tail:	Dark dun mayfly tails crimped
Body:	Hareline's Premo goose biots olive dun
Wing:	Zing Wing
Hackle:	Whiting's Blue-Winged Olive or equivalent
Thorax:	*Callibaetis* micro dry-fly dubbing

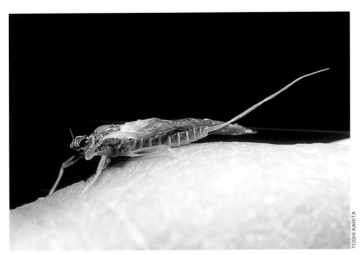

TOSHI KARITA

Drowned Dun

Hook:	Targus 101 or equivalent, size 14-22
Thread:	Match the color of the body
Tail:	Crimped mayfly tails
Body:	Micro tubing
Wing:	Zing Wing
Hackle:	Soft hackle
Thorax:	Micro dry-fly dubbing

On a trip to the Colorado River several years ago, Mike Bostwick and I found ourselves in a Trico hatch that we couldn't figure out. We tried duns, spinners and nymphs in sizes ranging from 18-24 but only ended up talking to ourselves. Filled with frustration, we began to slap the water with our dun patterns as we thought out loud to ourselves. Soon after, a few fish were on the end of our lines. We turned to each other, astonished with what had just transpired.

The duns were sinking and we were catching fish. This just didn't seem right, catching trout with sunken dry flies. Mike put on some split shot to get the fly down and he caught more big fish. This experience left an impression on us and hasn't been forgotten. The result is a series of flies, like the one demonstrated, to fill that void when all else fails.

When you stop and think about it, it makes sense. When the duns hatch in one flat area and drift through some rapids, some are naturally going to get damaged, or drowned, and thus picked off by fish. The main thing to remember is to make the wings lay back over the fly in a wet-fly style, and to never use stiff, high-quality hackle because this will float the fly. Another possibility is to use soft tailing fibers. You can use soft hackle or mallard flank if you wish, but here, I use hemostats and mayfly tails. The end result is a crippled-looking tail complete with segmentations that look damaged.

Put some split shot or other kind of weight on the fly in order to sink the Drowned Dun, and fish them like any other nymph pattern. It is especially effective when fished at tailouts in riffles because it is like a conveyer belt bringing food to fish in slack water. If you find that fish have started coming to the surface, and you do not have any regular duns, place some floatant on this fly and it will work well.

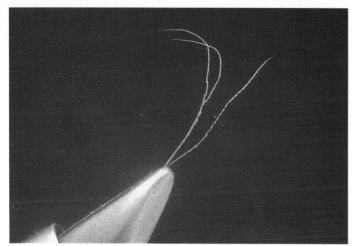

Step 1: Crimp three mayfly tails in the hemostats.

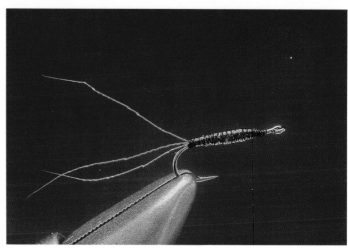

Step 2: Cut the tubing at an angle, then tie it in and wrap it forward. You should be 1/4 the way back from the hook eye.

Step 3: Tie in the hackle at the end of the body and the wings right behind the hook eye. Put a little bit of dubbing down in the thorax area.

Step 4: Pull the wings back and tie them down with your dubbed thread and dub the head area.

Step 5: Push the wings forward and take a turn of the hackle behind the wing. Push the wings back into place and continue wrapping the hackle forward. All that is needed are a couple of turns of the hackle if you want to leave it un-cut. If you are going to cut the hackle, as I have done here, a few more turns are suggested.

Top view.

MAYFLIES "TOP TO BOTTOM"

Drowned Dun, Tan

Hook:	Targus 101 or equivalent, size 14-22
Thread:	Tan
Tail:	Tan mayfly tails crimped
Body:	Tan micro tubing
Wing:	Zing Wing
Thorax:	*Callibaetis* micro dry-fly dubbing
Hackle:	Whiting's *Callibaetis* or equivalent

Drowned Dun, Olive

Hook:	Targus 101 or equivalent, size 14-22
Thread:	Olive
Tail:	Dark dun mayfly tails crimped
Body:	Olive micro tubing
Wing:	Zing Wing
Thorax:	*Callibaetis* micro dry-fly dubbing
Hackle:	Whiting's Blue-winged Olive or equivalent

Drowned Dun, Gray

Hook:	Targus 101 or equivalent, size 14-22
Thread:	Gray
Tail:	Dark dun mayfly tails crimped
Body:	Gray micro tubing
Wing:	Zing Wing
Thorax:	Gray micro dry-fly dubbing
Hackle:	Medium dun

Crippled Spinner

Hook:	Targus 101
Thread:	Match body color.
Tail:	Mayfly tails crimped
Body:	Micro tubing
Ribbing:	FisHair
Wing:	Zing wing
Shell back:	Medallion sheeting
Hackle:	Hen neck
Thorax:	Micro dry fly dubbing

A crippled spinner is a spinner that has sustained some type of injury. This can involve anything—from having a crooked tail to folded wings. Also the insect might still be fluttering its wings because they became wet before the insect wanted them to. No matter what the cause, these damaged insects are now prime targets for feeding fish.

Spinners are most often fished on slack water because that is where they end up. Plus, it's easier for anglers to fish these spots. When the spinner goes through a riffle and onto the slack water, it often incurs battle scars. The tails on artificials are crimped in the hemostats and the wings are tied so that they lay up, and back, like the wings of an emerger.

This design also gives the angler another opportunity to fish the fly in less than tranquil waters. Try fishing it as a wet fly through the riffles before you head to the pool. This may be the only stop you make. Once the wings of the spinner have touched the water's surface, it cannot take flight. It will become submerged on its journey through the rapids and will become easy pickings for the trout.

If you do make it to the pool below the riffle, do not change your fly. Sure it will be banged up a bit with the wings being split but this makes the fly an even more realistic representation of a cripple. The only change when fishing it as a wet fly is to add floatant.

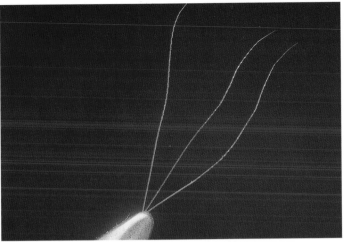

Step 1: Crimp three mayfly tails in a pair of hemostats.

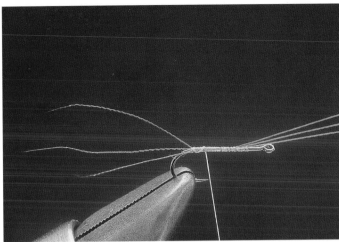

Step 2: Tie the tails in and then figure-eight through them so that they are separated.

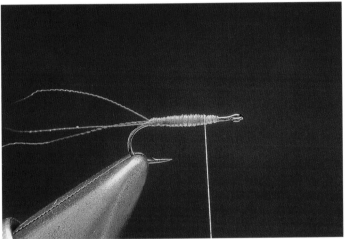

Step 3: Cut the tubing at an angle and tie it in by the tip. Tie in a piece of FisHair for the ribbing. Wrap the tubing forward and then rib it. You should be about 1/3 back from the hook eye.

Step 4: Tie in a piece of Medallion sheeting for the wing case, tie in a soft hackle, and then tie in the wings behind the hook eye.

Step 5: Dub the thorax and then wrap the hackle forward. Wind the thread back into the hackle and then pull the wings back and tie down. Make sure one wing is on top of the fly and the other is off to the side.

Step 6: Take the thread to the hook eye and then pull the wing case over the top and tie down and off. Pull the hackle fibers to the sides of the thorax. If any fibers still remain on the underside of the fly cut them off. You can also pinch it to make it flat.

Bottom view.

Top view.

Crippled Spinner, Tan

Hook:	Targus 101
Thread:	Tan
Tail:	Tan mayfly tails crimped
Body:	Tan micro tubing
Wing Case:	Tan Medallion sheeting
Wing:	Zing Wing
Hackle:	Whiting's *Callibaetis*
Thorax:	*Callibaetis* micro dry-fly dubbing

Crippled Spinner, Black

Hook:	Targus 101
Thread:	Black
Tail:	White mayfly tails crimped
Body:	Black micro tubing
Wing Case:	Dark dun Medallion sheeting
Wing:	Zing Wing
Hackle:	Black
Thorax:	Black micro dry-fly dubbing

Crippled Spinner, Olive

Hook:	Targus 101
Thread:	Olive
Tail:	Dark dun mayfly tails crimped
Body:	Olive micro tubing
Wing Case:	Medium dun Medallion sheeting
Wing:	Zing Wing
Hackle:	Whiting's Blue-Winged olive
Thorax:	*Callibaetis* micro dry-fly dubbing

INDEX

Contact Information

For information on any of these flies, or tying materials, contact:

Shane Stalcup
PO Box 211412
Denver, CO 80221

Or send e-mail to: dss@dimensional.com.

Many of these flies are distributed through Targus and the materials through Hareline Dubbin.

More Helpful Books for Fishing and Fly Tying

FEDERATION OF FLY FISHERS FLY PATTERN ENCYCLOPEDIA
Over 1600 of the Best Fly Patterns
Edited by Al & Gretchen Beatty

Simply stated, this book is a Federation of Fly Fishers' conclave taken to the next level, a level that allows the reader to enjoy the learning and sharing in the comfort of their own home. The flies, ideas, and techniques shared herein are from the "best of the best" demonstration fly tiers North America has to offer. The tiers are the famous as well as the unknown with one simple characteristic in common; they freely share their knowledge. Many of the unpublished patterns in this book contain materials, tips, tricks, or gems of information never before seen.

As you leaf through these pages, you will get from them just what you would if you spent time in the fly tying area at any FFF function. At such a show, if you dedicate time to observing the individual tiers, you can learn the information, tips, or tricks they are demonstrating. All of this knowledge can be found in *Federation of Fly Fishers Fly Pattern Encyclopedia* so get comfortable and get ready to improve upon your fly tying technique with the help of some of North America's best fly tiers. Full color, 8 1/2 x 11 inches, 232 pages.
SB: $39.95 ISBN: 1-57188-208-1

NEW YORK FLY FISHING GUIDE
Robert W. Streeter

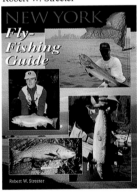

Mention New York and most people think: concrete, sirens, and yellow cabs. This is true of a small area, however the Empire State also includes big woods, wonderful rivers, crystal-clear lakes, and great fishing. In this book Rob shares: the state's moving and still waters; species you'll encounter; access; fly plates, histories of the famed waters of American fly-fishing pioneers Theodore Gordon and Lee Wulff; general regulations; effective presentations; extensive list of resources; and more. New York State fishing has a fascinating history, spectacular surroundings, and varied fisheries, if you are fortunate enough to live or visit there, let this book be your guide. 8 1/2 x 11 inches, 113 pages.
SB: $19.95 ISBN: 1-57188-157-3

STRIPER MOON
J. Kenney Abrames

This is a beautifully written, all-color book about coast wade fly fishing (near the shore) for striped bass. Abrames explains tides and baitfish and covers techniques, reading the water, and the flies to use (shown in color and with pattern dressings). The author has a deep love and understanding of the fishery and I guarantee that you will want to fly fish for these wonderful fish after you read it! 8 1/2 x 11 inches, 48 pages

SB: $15.95 ISBN: 1-878175-67-X

SALTWATER GAME FISHES OF THE WORLD
Bob Dunn and Peter Goadby

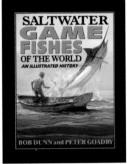

This is a book for all those who love the sea and the great oceanic and inshore fishes which inhabit it. It is a book, not only for anglers, but for marine scientists, nature lovers and seafarers of all nations who share a curiosity about these majestic creatures and how our knowledge of them slowly developed over the past two millennia. A 2000 year history of the early naturalist and fishes they first described. Illustrations are intensely evocative of the period and remind us of the skills of yesteryear, now largely lost. There is the never-told-before history of the ancient sport of sea fishing from its origins in the mists of antiquity to the present day. All color, 9.5 x 12.5 inches, 304 pages.

HB: $89.95 ISBN: 1-86513-010-9

VIRGINIA BLUE-RIBBON FLY FISHING GUIDE
Harry Murray

Virginia has a rich and vibrant history—President Hoover used to catch trout in the Blue Ridge Mountains to "wash his soul"—and a fishery to match it. The cool, clear waters of Virginia have much to offer the angler. Stream by stream, Harry Murray details their geography; the fish they hold; where and how to fish them; extensive resources; productive flies and presentations; and more. Virginia *is* for lovers—lovers of great angling in beautiful surroundings. 8 1/2 x 11 inches, 96 pages.
SB: $24.95 ISBN: 1-57188-159-X

HATCH GUIDE FOR NEW ENGLAND STREAMS
Thomas Ames, Jr.

New England's streams, and the insects and fish that inhabit them, have their own unique qualities. Their flowing waters support an amazing diversity of insect species from all of the major orders—in fact, at last count, Maine, alone, has 162 species of mayflies, the most of any state. Few, if any, books deal with the insects and life stages specific to New England, until now.

Hatch Guide to New England Streams, by professional photographer and "amateur entomology enthusiast" Thomas Ames, explores the insects of New England. Ames covers: reading water; presentations for New England streams; tackle; night fishing; and more. The bulk of this book, however, deals with the insects and the best flies to imitate them. Similar in style to Jim Schollmeyer's successful "Hatch Guide" series, Ames discusses the natural and its behaviors on the left-hand page and the three best flies to imitate it on the right, including proper size and effective techniques. Tom's color photography of the naturals and their imitations is superb, making this book as beautiful as it is useful. A must for all New England fly-fishers! Full color. 4 1/8 x 6 1/8 inches, 272 pages; insect and fly plates.
SB: $19.95 ISBN: 1-57188-210-3
HB: $29.95 ISBN: 1-57188-220-0

THE FLY TIER'S BENCHSIDE REFERENCE TO TECHNIQUES AND DRESSING STYLES
Ted Leeson and Jim Schollmeyer

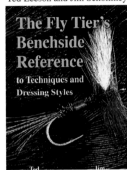

Printed in full color on top-quality paper, this book features over 3,000 color photographs and over 400,000 words describing and showing, step-by-step, hundreds of fly-tying techniques! Leeson and Schollmeyer have collaborated to produce this masterful volume which will be the standard fly-tying reference book for the entire trout-fishing world. Through enormous effort on their part they bring to all who love flies and fly fishing a wonderful compendium of fly-tying knowledge. Every fly tier should have this book in their library! All color, 8 1/2 by 11 inches, 464 pages, over 3,000 color photographs, index, hardbound with dust jacket.
HB: $100.00. ISBN: 1-57188-126-3

STRIPERS AND STREAMERS
Ray Bondorew
Introduction by Lefty Kreh

The striper is the ideal fish for the saltwater fly-rodder. In *Stripers and Streamers*, Bondorew shares his nearly forty years experience, giving us an in-depth look at what it takes to be a successful striped bass fly fisher, including: a history of both the sport and the fish, identifying the various water environs of stripers, proper presentations and flies, how paying special attention to the moon, wind, tides, current, and even the behaviors of birds and surfers, can provide clues to make you a well-informed striper fly fisher. *Stripers and Streamers* is the most up-to-date treatment of this fast-growing sport, with plenty for both beginner and expert alike! All-color, 5 1/2 x 8 1/2 inches, 120 pages.
SB: $19.95 ISBN: 1-57188-072-0

A PERFECT FISH
Ken Abrames

Take your fly tying a step further; not only will you catch more stripers and other game fish, but tying flies will take on a more personal and satisfying dimension for you, and as we all know confidence is the name of the game. Abrames shares: the freedom and creativity in fly design; techniques for successful fly fishing; many productive patterns and how to tie them; much information on game fish behavior; deep insight into stripers and the flies that catch them; and more.

Abrames introduces you to a whole new level in fly tying—harnessing your creativity and intelligence to make for more effective flies. 8 1/2 x 11 inches; 110 pages.
SB: $29.95 ISBN: 1-57188-138-7
HB: $39.95 ISBN: 1-57188-179-4

Ask for these books at your local fly/tackle shop or call toll-free to order:
1-800-541-9498 (8-5 p.s.t.) • www.amatobooks.com
Frank Amato Publications, Inc. • P.O. Box 82112 • Portland, Oregon 98282

0061